Saint Paul was Not Virgin Born

A study intended to humanize Paul of Tarsus and to honor Jesus of Nazareth

Ronald Lee Cobb

authorHOUSE®

AuthorHouse™
1663 Liberty Drive
Bloomington, IN 47403
www.authorhouse.com
Phone: 833-262-8899

Published by AuthorHouse 09/11/2020

ISBN: 978-1-7283-5927-4 (sc)
ISBN: 978-1-7283-5928-1 (hc)
ISBN: 978-1-7283-5926-7 (e)

Library of Congress Control Number: 2020917000

Print information available on the last page.

This book is printed on acid-free paper.

Scripture quotations marked MSG are taken from THE MESSAGE. Copyright
© 1993, 1994, 1995, 1996, 2000, 2001, 2002, 2003 by Eugene H. Peterson.
Used by permission of NavPress Publishing Group. Website.

To
Dan Maltby,

whose dedication
to Jesus of Nazareth,
to Paul of Tarsus, and
to helping the poor
and feeding the hungry
has forever changed my soul

Saint is the correct word for Paul of Tarsus. He can rightly be compared to Abraham, Moses, Elijah, John the Baptist, Peter the Rock, and Saint Francis of Assisi. Throughout his voluminous writings Paul consistently states that he is simply the messenger, "the least of the Apostles." Jesus of Nazareth is to Paul the Son of the Living God, the human image of God, the Creator of the Cosmos, and the resurrected Redeemer. It is all about Jesus.

CONTENTS

CHAPTER 1

With Paul, It Was Always All about Jesus

In every single one of the epistles that were indisputably written by Paul, it is always all about Jesus. Yet there is no question that even though Paul had a strong ego, he consistently tried to put it aside and make it only about Jesus of Nazareth.

One of the reasons Paul consistently points to Jesus was that he was aware enough of himself, unlike many narcissistic people, to realize that he had to battle with his giant ego daily. He used the energy from fighting his dark side to focus on Jesus and on helping others in his life who were also trying to follow the Master from Galilee.

In addition to having a massive ego, Paul was obsessive-compulsive. He was obsessed with getting the message out that Jesus was more than a Nazarene, that Jesus was indeed the long-awaited Messiah come in the flesh. He wanted others to know that Jesus was not an earthly messiah to liberate Judah from the Romans but something greater, a Messiah to liberate people from sin, guilt, and shame and to change their lives from those of scriptural scholarship and religious rites to ones of vibrant personal inner peace and joy.

Being obsessive-compulsive is a strength as well as a weakness. Brain surgeons need to be obsessive-compulsive, and the Greek medical doctor named Luke was also blessed with obsessive-compulsive tendencies. Luke systematically interviewed many people, including Mary, the Mother of Jesus, and took notes in precise detail before he wrote his gospel, and he did indeed write a wonderful, historical, and accurate gospel. Paul was his mentor in following Jesus, and he recorded Paul's life well.

Paul was also a mystic. He believed in dreams and visions. The man in a dream calling him to come to Macedonia had a vivid reality to him. Too few Christians in the twenty-first century are open to experiences like this. The Macedonian dream itself was all about Jesus, about telling the "Good News" about Jesus to people in Greece, Europe, and elsewhere who had never heard.

Paul was viewed by the Greeks and Romans as a religious fanatic, as one of the leaders of a "Jewish sect" called Christians or Nazarenes. Paul was much more than this; he was a man who had been met face-to-face with Jesus and Jesus's power, grace, healing, and peace.

Many have posited that Paul's energy sprang primarily from guilt and shame because he had so heavily persecuted the early followers of Jesus. Paul does talk about his guilt, but the primary driver of his life was love and gratitude and being all about Jesus.

In over two thousand years of church history, it is so obvious that many people who thought they were following Jesus, in reality, were too often following a religious system or a corner of the Christian faith set up by some other follower of Jesus. Other times, they were following rules and regulations that initially were about Jesus but became about religious observances. Paul and the early Jewish believers and Gentile Christians were all about experiencing the power, presence, and teachings of Jesus in their own lives.

Over the centuries, Christian belief systems gradually replaced personal experiences. In fact, repeatedly, when others reported they were experiencing God personally, that idea was often viewed by religious leaders as dangerous to the church structure and questionable because it might introduce heresy into Christianity. Intimate experiences with God were often shunned and denied in the past and still are right up to today. People who create structures tend to be anxious, and their anxiety wants nothing to do with anything outside their precise structure.

This is understandable, yet the reality is that one person with a personal experience is worth more than one hundred people with a theory. This experiential reality is a powerful fact that exhibits itself in society, businesses, homes, medicine, academia, and every aspect of life itself. Paul of Tarsus's life was full of numerous encounters with the risen Jesus of Nazareth that gave him energy, wisdom, and vitality beyond any rigid belief system.

Jesus has too often been replaced by one of the twelve disciples, one of his family members, or some other Christian saint. People who do this often have a deep faith in God, but they can lose their focus that the Christian life is all about Jesus. I have been too close to making too much of St. Francis of Assisi; Padre Pio (my favorite saint); the Cur du Ares (my second favorite saint); or some anointed twenty-first-century television pastor, priest, or teacher. It is easy to forget that the Christian life is all about Jesus.

Paul's driving force needs to be the driving force of every Christian. I would encourage you as you read these words to make your Christian life always *all about Jesus*. Jesus was all about helping everyone find the will of God for his or her life. He wanted all those he touched to know that they belonged in the world, that they were special, and that they were loved by God personally.

CHAPTER 2

Abram to Abraham, Simon to Peter, and Saul to Paul

Names in Hebrew have very powerful meanings. Abram was changed to Abraham, which means "a great multitude," because of his faithfulness to God. It is also awesome that Saul the Pharisee, who sat at the feet of Gamliel, became Paul, an apostle of Jesus.

The problem is that because of the overemphasis on Paul in many churches, too many Christians fail to see that name changes and vocational changes also occurred with all the other disciples who served God. Andrew, who did not believe that anything good could come out of Nazareth, changed his mind immediately when he first encountered Jesus. Fishermen no longer fished. Tax collectors no longer took taxes. Haters of Gentiles who wanted to separate themselves from all non-Jews became friends of those Greek, Syrian, and other outsiders who wanted to follow Jesus of Nazareth.

Thomas the doubter became Thomas the believer; Simon the Zealot became much less warlike and more peaceful; and James and John, the "Sons of Thunder," no longer had any desire to burn up villages that did not accept Jesus. Paul is special in that his name was changed, but all the other disciples whose names and lives changed are special too. Jesus made it clear that every person who followed him because of their testimony was also special. You are special.

The Hebrew scriptures and the Christian scriptures are incredibly honest about the flaws of Abraham, Isaac, Jacob, Elijah, and David. Paul of Tarsus continued this honesty in his epistles, writing about his own flaws. Such honesty proves the authenticity of Paul and of the entire Bible.

CHAPTER 3

Ananias, a Follower of Jesus of Nazareth Too Often Forgotten

In chapter 9 of the book of Acts, there is a wonderful story about Ananias, a follower of Jesus of Nazareth in Damascus. Paul had a vision of an incredibly bright light, heard a thundering voice, and discovered that the voice was the voice of Jesus of Nazareth, whom he was "persecuting." Paul was temporarily blinded and had to be led to the home of a Jewish friend from Tarsus who was living in Damascus.

God then spoke to Ananias in a vision and told him to go over to Straight Street, to the house of Judas, Paul's friend from Tarsus, Paul's hometown, and ask for Saul. Ananias reluctantly obeyed. Paul had a bad reputation with Christians.

A street by that exact name, Straight Street, as mentioned earlier, still exists in Damascus. It is the main road the Romans used and runs from east to west through the old city. In Arabic, its name is الشارع المستقيم or *Al-Shāri' al*-Mustaqīm in Latin letters. God told Ananias that Paul was praying and had just had a vision in which he had seen a man named Ananias enter the house and lay hands on him to restore his sight.

Ananias protested, resisting God's directions, and replied, "Master, you can't be serious. Everybody's talking about this man, the terrible things he's been doing, and his reign of terror against your people in Jerusalem! And now he's shown up here with papers from the chief priest that give him license to do the same to us."

But God told him, "Don't argue. Go! I have picked him as my personal representative to non-Jews and kings and Jews. And now I'm about to show him what he's in for—the hard suffering that goes with this job."

Ananias was obedient in spite of realistic fears for his own life. He "went and found the house, placed his hands on blind Saul, and said, 'Brother Saul, the Master sent me, the same Jesus you saw on your way here. He sent me so you could see again and be filled with the Holy Spirit.'" As soon as Ananias spoke, "Something like scales fell from Saul's eyes—he could see again! He got to his feet, was baptized, and sat down with them to a hearty meal."

This oft-forgotten man, Ananias, put his life on the line to obey God. Every believer in Jesus of Nazareth as the Messiah needs to have much gratitude for Ananias and his close walk with God. He was so sensitive that the Holy Spirit could speak directly to him about Paul.

Ananias was a totally obedient follower of Jesus of Nazareth who was willing to put his life on the line to obey God. He realized that if he was open enough to hearing God speak directly to him, even if it did not seem logical, then he must obey. This is the serious responsibility that goes along with being a Christian and having a deep spiritual life and a heart sensitive to the Holy Spirit's direction. Ananias was totally sold out to following God. Too often, he is forgotten in the story of Paul's life.

CHAPTER 4

Paul of Tarsus and Barnabas, the Forgiver and the Encourager

Paul was an unstoppable force as a believer in Damascus and Jerusalem, just like he had been an unstoppable force as a persecutor of Christians. Remember that you and I would not be believers if it were not for Paul and his unstoppable dedication to his new Master, Jesus of Nazareth. It was Paul's nature to be all or nothing. He was the perfect tool to spread the Good News of God's love through Jesus of Nazareth.

Paul's faith that Jesus was the Messiah for whom the Jewish people and the entire world had waited for so many centuries drove him on and on. (To this day, the followers of the Shiite version of Islam, whose center is in what used to be ancient Persia or Iran, still wait for a messiah or Madhab.)

So we see Barnabus as another too often hidden hero. He was clearly a beloved person in the early church, similar in nature to the apostle John, Jesus's closest friend. Barnabus was a quiet hero, a kind, compassionate, and forgiving person.

In Acts 4:36, we see that Barnabus's birth name was Joseph and that he was a "Levite from Cyprus." The Christians in Jerusalem gave him a nickname, Varnava, which means he was an encourager, one who calls people to work closer together in emotionally intimate relationships. In other words, Barnabus was a peacemaker. His name is taken from the Greek word *parakaleo*, which is the same Greek word for the Holy Spirit. "Son of Encouragement" was the basic meaning of his nickname to the Christians of the church in Jerusalem. Barnabus, similar to Ananias, also put "his life on the line" for Paul, so in that sense, he is truly heroic.

Most Christians in Jerusalem were still afraid of Paul—afraid he would throw them into prison like he had so many other Christians. At first, it is important to remember that Barnabus was dealing with a rather youthful Paul of Tarsus. The intensity of youth magnified Paul's already intense personality.

In Acts 15, we learn that later on in Paul's Christian evangelistic journeys, because of a sharp disagreement about Mark, Barnabus and Paul split. The reason for the disagreement was that in Antioch, Paul would not allow Mark to go with them. Earlier Paul felt Mark had "abandoned" him on one of his mission trips in Pamphylia. Barnabus then reconciled with Mark, left Paul, and went with him to Cyprus, and Paul took Silas and went to Syria.

The Hellenists, with whom Paul was keeping up a running verbal battle, were Greeks who had become Jews. These

Greeks spoke no Aramaic. Their mother tongue was Greek. They were sometimes called God-Fearers and were converts to Judaism.

"Hellenists," as Greek Jewish converts, often adopted things from Greek culture that were not Jewish. This trait sometimes made them at odds with both Jews and Christians. Their Greek culture could very well have been one of many complicated issues related to Paul and Mark parting. Paul was arguing with the Hellenists about several things around the central issue that Jesus was indeed the long-awaited Messiah. With Paul, it was always all about Jesus.

Note, Acts 15 describes how in Damascus, the church continued to grow after Paul left, and in Jerusalem, the church continued to "prosper wonderfully." Even though there are controversies, personalities, and disagreements in any modern church, God's work will still continue to prosper and grow. Let us all strive to be like Barnabus, an encourager, and to reconcile Christians to work with other Christians. Then the Paraklete, the Spirit of God, will be with us just as God was with Barnabus, the peacemaker.

CHAPTER 5

Cain, Herod, Assad, Putin, ISIS, and Paul

One thing that constantly amazes me is that so many Christians in the Western world who worship the God of Jesus of Nazareth and the God who is Jesus of Nazareth have no idea about the actual boots-on-the-ground realities that have been going on since the beginning of time in the Middle East. The incredible violence in this "cradle of civilization" between all the cultures of the Nile River Valley and the Mesopotamian River Valley is much more bloodthirsty than many in the West can possibly imagine.

As a retired colonel in the US Army, I have been privy to some of the bloodiest, cruelest, and most diabolical military behaviors imaginable. They went far beyond the Geneva Conventions. These heinous acts never make any major newspapers in the world because of their sheer brutality. As hardened as I have had to become to survive thirty years in the US Army, knowing this, I am leaving these grotesque stories out of this book. The inhumanity of humans to other humans is focused more cruelly than that of any carnivore who is simply trying to survive by killing and eating another animal.

Command and General Staff College and the Naval Postgraduate School for International Relations courses and my intense study of military history have taught me that Cain's actions, Herod's actions, Assad's actions, Putin's actions, and the violence of ISIS and the Islamic State in Syria are not isolated instances. They are systemic problems and social realities in the Middle East and in the entire world. Paul knew the highest moral values of Greek Stoicism and Gamaliel's Judaism, yet he was also the son of the "law of the jungle" type of violence in that corner of the world.

Cain, out of jealousy, sibling rivalry, and anger, slaughtered his own brother, Seth. King Herod did not hesitate in killing every male child who was two years of age or younger in and around Bethlehem when he found that a potential king, Jesus, had been recently born there. Hafez al-Assad, father of Bashar al-Assad, had no hesitation in killing every man, woman, and child in a rebellious Syrian village and leveling it to the ground with bulldozers. You cannot even see where the rather large village existed today.

Vladimir Putin has shown no hesitation in openly assassinating large numbers of Russian journalists in the beginning of the twenty-first century when they questioned even his smallest executive decision. The Islamic State in Syria (ISIS) systematically murdered anyone who was not a believer in radical Islam, taking thousands of lives of moderate followers of Islam, Yazidis, Mandaeans, Jews, Hindus, and Christians.

Paul of Tarsus was a child of his time, of his neighborhood, and of his culture, a culture that has always existed in Syria, the Middle East, and the world. Paul actually was in Syria on the road to Damascus when his life was turned around. From arresting and approving the murder of Christians, he became one of the most well-known apostles of Jesus of Nazareth, after only Peter and John. When Paul was blinded by the Shekinah glory of God, he was told to go to a house on Straight Street in Damascus as mentioned earlier. This corner of the world has many civilized, kind, urbane people and at the very same time still has tribes, violence, and animosity stretching clear back before recorded civilization. Today, we cannot judge Paul of Tarsus by his behaviors. He lived in that culture and that type of world. We cannot judge him by twenty-first-century Geneva Convention standards.

CHAPTER 6

Paul Was Plowing Straight into the Opposition

Paul was indeed an unstoppable force as a Jewish purist, and so he naturally tended to be an unstoppable force after he became a follower of Jesus of Nazareth. This is very clear in Acts 9:19–25. Paul didn't seem to have an "off" button. After he got acquainted with the followers of Jesus of Nazareth in Damascus, he knew the Hebrew scriptures so well that he "wasted no time" and immediately went into all the Jewish meeting places (Synagogues) trying to convince them that Jesus was the Son of God. He did this for quite a long time.

Luke, the author of the book of Acts, graphically describes him: "He plowed straight into the opposition." There is an Old English saying, "One convinced against his will becometh unconvinced still." There is also Jesus's teaching that if a village or a person doesn't accept the Good News to "shake the dust off your feet" and go on to the next village. In other words, don't waste your time. Paul kept on pushing against any opposition.

Paul wrote the first books in the New Testament. The gospels were written after Paul began to write, so he might not have even read or heard of the words of Jesus advising that when someone doesn't accept your message, you should move on and to "shake the dust off your feet."

The things that Jesus had taught at the time Paul was in Damascus were still oral traditions from eyewitnesses. Jesus's disciples and followers remembered many of his actions and teachings, but it was initially an oral tradition. Jesus's history, words, and life were written down later, approximately between thirty and one hundred years after his birth and resurrection after of Paul's epistles.

I can't imagine Peter or any of the other followers of Jesus at that time except Paul so strongly taking on the opposition—primarily Jews who did not believe that Jesus was the Messiah. These Jews did not appreciate Paul stealing Gentile converts and Jews from their synagogues. I don't think even brash James and John would have done what Paul did. That is also to Paul's credit. He was fearless.

I can't imagine any of Jesus's followers taking on every single congregation in every one of the Jewish synagogues that existed then in Damascus. These synagogues were full of established scholars and scribes, but Paul took them on over and over again.

Paul's intensity and directness were his great strength as well as one of his greatest burdens. It appears that at times Paul was needlessly relentless, but this is also what made him the one leader in the early church who brought the message of Jesus to the non-Jewish world. We would not be Christians today but for Paul of Tarsus.

Paul reminds me of an early American evangelist named Billy Sunday. Billy had been a boxer in his youth, and sometimes, his sermons showed it. Billy was aggressive like Paul. One of his statements in the rough American Midwest of his day was "If I ever met the devil, I'd hit him until I had no more fists. Then I'd bite him until I had no more teeth. Then I'd gum him to death." Obviously, Billy had a sense of humor. As a young apostle in Damascus, Paul didn't seem to have much of a sense of humor.

Paul therefore proved to be both a blessing and a curse to those early Christians. There is an ancient Jewish wisdom teaching in Proverbs 14:4 that basically says,

> There is much strength in an ox but
> you have to clean out the stable
> where the ox is kept.

Reading the book of Acts, one realizes that many Christians in Damascus were relieved in two ways when they let Paul down from the city wall to freedom because angry people from several Damascus synagogues were actively plotting to murder him. The Damascus Christians were relieved, first, that Paul was safe and second, that when Paul left the city of Damascus, the rhetoric would calm down and therefore they would be in less danger of being murdered themselves and having their own places of worship destroyed.

Paul had stirred up the Jews who did not believe in Jesus so much that they sat at every single city gate in Damascus seeking to assassinate him. If they murdered Paul, they could very well do the same to other Damascus believers. To save Paul and to save themselves, the Damascus Christians lowered Paul in a basket over the wall away from the gates so he could escape.

CHAPTER 7

What Kind of Man Was
This Paul of Tarsus?

As we unmistakably see in Acts 9, Paul was a real handful for the Jewish believers in Jerusalem as well. There is nothing wrong with being an obsessive-compulsive follower of Jesus if you know you tend to be obsessive, but at this point, as a young man and a young believer, Paul's faith and personality were only in the beginning stages of being formed.

You and I are often so like Paul. We try to love God, and yet our love is limited by our human understanding. We all are a mixture of good and bad. The secret to this dilemma can be found in Paul's life. Keep your eyes on Jesus of Nazareth, whom Paul loved with all his heart, soul, mind, and strength. Paul was *all about Jesus*.

Paul reminds us of the words of an early twentieth-century Christian hymn: "Keep your eyes upon Jesus. Look full in his wonderful face, and the things of earth will grow strangely dim, in the light of his glory and grace." This is the major theme of this chapter and of this book. It is all about Jesus. Paul's letters and life prove beyond any doubt that he wholeheartedly would approve this Jesus-centered stance and would wholeheartedly agree that he, Paul of Tarsus, needed to be seen as Jesus's follower, not as Jesus's alter ego. *It was all about Jesus.*

CHAPTER 8

Luke the Physician, Saul the Zealot, and Paul the Apostle

After the foundational stories of Jesus in the four gospels of Matthew, Mark, Luke, and John, Paul's message, personality, and history cover literally more than half of the pages of the Christian New Testament.

Luke starts recording the life of Paul in the book of Acts of the Apostles. After the first few chapters, Acts is all about Paul of Tarsus. Luke faithfully records that Paul's life from beginning to end was all about Jesus of Nazareth. Luke the Physician was obviously an eyewitness of many of the stories about Paul told in the book of Acts. He was most assuredly Paul's traveling companion during the shipwreck on Malta and Paul's last journey to Rome.

Paul wrote the majority of the New Testament epistles or letters. No wonder he remains a primary source of authority on Jesus of Nazareth and the majority of the earliest Christian history. Paul had such strength of personality, such brilliance of intellect, and such commanding oratory that he had to have had an incredibly powerful influence.

CHAPTER 9

Luke; Mary, the Mother of Jesus; and Paul

When we were in Ephesus, we walked down the sloping main street of the ancient city. Surprisingly intact stone structures were to our left and right. At the bottom of the avenue were the remains of what used to be the third largest library in the Roman Empire. Then the avenue turned to the right, and we walked past the huge amphitheater in the hillside of Ephesus.

We stopped. Our guide asked us to turn and said, "Look up on the hill. Do you see that cleared area? That is where Mary, the Mother of Jesus, is buried. Pope John Paul II came here and went up to her grave and sat there for two hours and had communion there a few years ago." Few Christians are aware of the location of Mary's grave. Mary fades from the memory of many people after the death and resurrection of Jesus. Her gravesite jarred me.

We had already been to the location of the house where Mary in her old age had been cared for by John the Apostle. Remember on the cross when Mary and John were standing before Jesus, and before he died, he said, "Mother, behold thy son" (John 19:26 KJV). He was telling John to care for his mother after he was gone. John was faithful to that task. When he was sent to the Isle of Patmos, his followers undoubtedly continued caring for Mary. What a wonderful story about Mary and John, Jesus's beloved disciple, in the Gospel of John.

The Gospel of Luke begins with the intimate story of Elizabeth, the high priest Zachariah, and the birth of John the Baptist. There are so many details it very probably was told to Luke by Mary herself. Next, Luke records many personal details about Mary's long visit with Elizabeth that had to have been first-person stories. Then he shares Zachariah's prophesy and blessing on his newborn son, John the Baptist. Next, in chapter 2, Luke tells many details about the birth of Jesus, the visit of the shepherds, and Simeon and the prophetess Anna in the temple giving their blessings to the eight-day-old Jesus— amazing and detailed eyewitness stories that only Mary could tell. In Luke 2:34–35 MSG, Simeon turns, looks directly at Mary, and says,

> This child marks both the failure and the recovery of many in Israel, A figure misunderstood and contradicted—the pain of a sword-thrust through you—But the rejection will force honesty, as God reveals who they really are.

Next, Luke tells the only story of Jesus's youth in any of the gospels, where Jesus, at twelve years of age, astounds the wise teachers of the Law in the temple in Jerusalem with his questions and discussions with them. Eighteen years later, when he began his ministry as an adult, there were some of them who had to have thought, *Wait. Look at him and his words. This is the same man who years ago at such a young age amazed us at his insights.*

Paul never met Jesus of Nazareth, but through Luke, he knew him well from the incredible, detailed stories of Luke's gospel. We will never know if Paul ever met or spoke with Jesus's mother, Mary, but through Luke and the twelve disciples, there is no question but that Paul was well acquainted with the teachings of her son, Jesus of Nazareth, and Paul *was all about Jesus.*

CHAPTER 10

Paul of Tarsus, "A Force of Nature"

There was another repeated insight that consistently emerged as I studied Paul for the past fifty years. Paul's words and presence and teachings I can only call "a force of nature." Paul's intensity leaps off the pages of the epistles that he wrote to the new churches he had helped found and to other churches he planned to visit. The breadth of his missionary journeys and his desire to evangelize Iberia (Spain) also speak of his vision and his force of personality.

Paul also spoke several languages, at the very least Greek, Latin, Aramaic, and Hebrew. His dynamic personality, his words, and his message about Jesus of Nazareth all mean Paul was able to be clearly understood by the people whom he was evangelizing.

In my intense study of the classical Greek Stoic philosophers, it became crystal clear to me that Paul had not only read the Stoics but also approved of their content and had a deep understanding of their ethical and philosophical guidelines (see the chapter on the Stoics). Paul later studied under Gamaliel, one of the most urbane, learned, and magnanimous teachers in the history of Israel, who taught in the City of Jerusalem (see the chapter on Gamaliel).

Luke's faith story and life story were intimately connected with Paul of Tarsus. At first, Luke wrote of Paul the misguided, religiously addicted sinner. As previously mentioned, after beginning the Acts of the Apostles, Luke shifts the focus from the twelve Jewish apostles in Jerusalem to Paul of Tarsus the apostle and to the Gentiles and non-Jews throughout the entire Roman Empire.

Luke intentionally emphasizes Stephen's message of faith and gracious forgiveness as he was stoned to death prior to Paul's face-to-face meeting with Jesus of Nazareth's light and voice on the road to Damascus. Both the sequence of events and Luke's writings on Paul of Tarsus set the scene for any reader of the Christian scripture.

Coming now to the forefront of the Christian movement through history, Luke is saying, is this man, this Saul and then Paul. This man from Tarsus was going to become another Jesus-like apostle, prophet, evangelist, pastor, and teacher, and Luke never failed to mention that Paul of Tarsus was *all about Jesus of Nazareth*.

CHAPTER 11

Comparing the Apostle Peter to the Apostle Paul

When we compare the Apostle Peter to the Apostle Paul, we can see several things that could be regarded as placing Peter in a more favorable light than Paul. Peter received his name change in a face-to-face, flesh-and-blood, eye-to-eye encounter with the living Jesus. In spite of Peter's temporary lapses of faith, he was true to his calling to be one of the most solid rocks of faith in the historical Jerusalem church.

In contrast, Paul initially struggled against the "goads" or "pricks" of his conscience. Paul held Stephen's clothing while the other zealots stoned him to death. Paul saw the first deacon, Stephen, die a majestic death paraphrasing the same words of Jesus on the cross: "God, please do not hold this against them. They don't know what they are doing." Yet Paul continued to persecute Christians in the name of Pharisaical Judaism and the name of the Sadducees. Paul congratulated those who had stoned Stephen to death. Still, it was hard for

Paul to go against the "goad" of his own inner sense of right and wrong.

Paul never personally knew Jesus of Nazareth face to face. The book of the Acts of the Apostles, by this Greek physician named Luke and full of Greek medical terms, is obviously written to magnify and amplify the life and works of Paul. Yet Luke is very honest about the fact that Paul was fighting against his own conscience. The light from heaven was a huge wakeup call. Many Christians have placed Paul on a loftier throne than the apostle Peter. They are both important, and Paul repeatedly says this himself in his own letters to the churches.

Neither the apostle Peter nor the apostle Paul was greater than the other. They had separate gifts. Peter's gift was to stabilize the mainly Jewish Christians in the church in Jerusalem and bear witness to the Jewish community there. Paul's gift was to be the apostle or "sent one" to the Greeks and Romans and other "outsiders" throughout the Mediterranean world.

It may be significant that Saul means "asked for" and that his name was changed to Paul, which means "little." Perhaps Paul and the Good Lord who changed his name were alluding in his new name that he was in fact what he called himself, "The least of the [twelve] Apostles."

CHAPTER 12

The Seven Sons of Sceva, Jesus Is Greater than Paul

In the seven sons of Sceva scenario, the author of Acts 19, Dr. Luke, records an interesting story. As a medical doctor, Luke dealt with both physical illnesses and related mental health disorders. This is what every general practitioner, every medical doctor, also does today. Luke makes it clear that Jesus, the Master, is the source of power and that God, through Jesus and Paul, healed both body and soul. The demons had to leave in Jesus's name:

> *Some itinerant Jewish exorcists who happened to be in town at the time tried their hand at what they assumed to be the "game" that Paul was playing (casting out demons) They pronounced the name of the Master Jesus over victims of evil spirits, saying, "I command you by the Jesus preached by Paul!" They were the seven sons of Sceva, the Jewish High Priest. They were trying to do this on a man when the evil spirit talked*

> *back: "I know Jesus and I have heard of Paul,*
> *but who are you?" (Acts 19:13–15 MSG)*

When we read closely the words that Luke wrote about this interesting and dynamic episode, we see that the demons clearly "know" Jesus and to a lesser degree "have heard of Paul." Luke is telling this story advisably. The words of the demons show Jesus as the Master and make Paul as Jesus's servant, a lesser figure. Luke lists this hierarchy—Jesus first, Paul second—in both his gospel and in his book of the Acts of the Apostles. Paul also says this in his epistles. Paul would have it no other way. It was all about Jesus. Paul was trying to be a faithful servant to Jesus of Nazareth.

> *Then the possessed man went berserk—*
> *jumped the exorcists, beat them up, and tore*
> *off their clothes. Naked and bloody, they got*
> *away as best they could. It was soon news all*
> *over Ephesus among both Jews and Greeks.*
> *The realization spread that God was in and*
> *behind this. Curiosity about Paul developed*
> *into reverence for the Master Jesus. (Acts*
> *19:16 MSG)*

Paul repeatedly said that he was simply a servant of Jesus. Luke consistently points out that the "curiosity" of the demons attacking the exorcists led people to develop a reverence for the source of the power, "the Master Jesus." Paul was simply a messenger of that power. These are key, foundational words to understanding the intent of this book: "Curiosity about Paul developed into *reverence for the Master Jesus*."

> *Many of those who thus believed came out of the closet and made a clean break with their secret sorceries. All kinds of witches and warlocks came out of the woodwork with their books of spells and incantations and made a huge bonfire of them. Some estimated their work at fifty thousand silver coins. In such ways it became evident that the Word of the Master was now sovereign and prevails in Ephesus. (Acts 19:18–20 MSG)*

CHAPTER 13

Magic, Witchcraft, and Fortune-Telling Now and Then

Throughout history right up to the present, virtually every culture around the world has its shamans, magic, spell-makers, and witches teaching various incantations. At the publication of this book, witches and open witchcraft itself are growing in the Western world. It was the same in those days as well as all centuries.

There are many ancient examples. Even the making of Easter eggs comes from pre-Hebrew, pre-Christian Egyptian superstition. The population of the Nile River Valley believed that if every spring they hung colored eggs on Egyptian temples, they would be protected from the "evil eye." This custom spread to the entire Mediterranean world and still exists today.

On Easter Sunday, when my wife and I were in Tuzla, Bosnia-Herzegovina, an Islamic couple who were friends and owned a wonderful restaurant gave Kathleen and me two Easter eggs. One was a yellow Easter egg with a cross on it, and the other was a green Easter egg with the crescent of Islam on it. Radical Islamists hate this custom, but it still exists today. Few followers of Islam or of Jesus of Nazareth know this custom comes right out of ancient Egyptian superstition and magical thinking.

After teaching many college classes on world religions for years, I still am consistently amazed to see that this superstitious, magical thinking continues to occur not only in non-Abrahamic religions but even within the apparently more staid Roman Catholic, Protestant, and Islamic cultures and faith groups of many different countries. It exists in the pagan, occult ceremonies of Voodoo, in the Day of the Dead in Latin America, and in the celebration of Halloween. Today, magical spells and incantations also continue to exist side by side with many other religions, such as Hinduism, Buddhism, Taoism, Zoroastrianism, Shintoism, and virtually every current and ancient animistic faith group.

In the last verses of the Acts 19 passage, Luke points out—and I want to emphasize Luke's phrase again—that because of the power of God in casting out demons, *the Word of the Master was now sovereign and prevails in Ephesus.* It was not the word of Paul. It was *the Word of the Master.* It was all about Jesus. It was all about the fact that Jesus is Lord or, put in the MSG translation of this passage, Jesus is *the Master. It is all about Jesus.*

CHAPTER 14

Stephen Forgives and Blesses Saul and Those Who Stoned Him to Death

What would have happened to Saul (later known as Paul) if Stephen had not forgiven him and the other men who stoned him to death? Would Paul have become a believer in Jesus as Messiah without hearing Stephen's blessing and forgiveness? Stephen's initial words in Acts 7 (MSG) right before he was stoned to death were very intense words of justified anger, which were prophetically honest, insultingly true, and very candid:

> *"And you continue, so bullheaded! Calluses on your hearts, flaps on your ears! Deliberately ignoring the Holy Spirit. You are just like your ancestors. Was there ever a prophet who didn't get the same treatment? Your ancestors killed anyone who dared talk about the coming of the Just One. You have kept up the family tradition— traitors and murderers, all of you. You had God's Law handed to you by angels—gift wrapped*

and you squandered it!" At that point they went wild, a rioting mob of catcalls and whistles and invective. But Stephen, full of the Holy Spirit, hardly noticed—he only had eyes for God, whom he saw in all his glory with Jesus standing at his side. He said, "Oh! I see heaven wide open and the Son of Man standing at God's side!" Yelling and hissing, the mob drowned him out. Now in full stampede, they dragged him out of town and belted him with rocks. The ringleaders took off their coats and asked a young man named Saul to watch them. As the rocks rained down, Stephen prayed, "Master Jesus take my life." Then he knelt down, praying loud enough for everyone to hear, "Master, don't blame them for this sin"—his last words. Then he died. Saul was right there, congratulating the killers. (Acts 7:51–53 MSG)

Paul was an up-close-and-personal eyewitness to Stephen's words as he was stoned to death. Paul's initial reaction was to "congratulate the killers," as mentioned earlier. Later, Paul began his own campaign of finding, persecuting, and arresting Christians.

Would Paul have become a believer of "the Way" and a follower of Jesus without being a coconspirator in Stephen's death? Would he have accepted God's forgiveness and forgiven himself if he had not personally heard Stephen's words of forgiveness and blessing? Almost assuredly, no.

There can be no question that Stephen's words resonated in Paul's subconscious mind more than he was willing to admit for a long time. Stephen's earlier honest and angry words about Paul's ancestors and their rejection of God's prophets later also most assuredly had to have deeply impacted on Paul's subconscious. They had to have touched the depths of Paul's soul as the road to Damascus graphically shows.

Stephen's forgiveness and his request for God not to "blame" those who were murdering him also had to have especially sunk down deep into Paul. Paul, in part, became a believer because of Stephen's last words. Years later, Paul and others surely told Dr. Luke his version of Stephen's death and Stephen's words. Luke wrote them in detail in the "Acts of the Apostles."

Over the years, Stephen's last words became even more meaningful and relevant to Paul. In Paul's later years and before his death at the hands of the Romans, I am certain that by then, Stephen's words and his shining, Shekinah-glory face as he was dying made Paul's forgiveness an even more blessed reality. Paul had accepted God's forgiveness. Then Paul had learned how to forgive himself, since both Stephen and Jesus made this very clear right before they both died. These words transformed into something even more sublime and precious to Paul as he faced his own death in Rome. Paul realized *it was all about Jesus.*

CHAPTER 15

Paul's Two Cousins, Andronicus and Junias

In Romans 16:7 (MSG), Paul says, "Say hello to my cousins Andronicus and Junias. We once shared a jail cell. They were believers in Christ before I was. Both of them are outstanding leaders." Andronicus and Junia were followers of Jesus before Paul. Many Christians gloss over this fact. I have read that passage many times before as well until their two names leaped off the page to me. The implications of Paul's words are enormous. Their faith in Jesus had to have had a huge effect on Paul's life.

After he became a follower of Jesus of Nazareth, Paul probably had even closer ties with his cousins, his nephew, and his extended family members who were believers. When his nephew in Jerusalem heard Jewish zealots discuss their plot to assassinate Paul when he was a prisoner, as described in Acts 23, he immediately went and told Paul. Paul asked one of the Roman centurions to take his nephew to the Roman army captain. The Roman army then protected Paul. His nephew saved his life.

We know from reading all of Paul's writings that he was not simply a totally hard-hearted, unthinking zealot who callously arrested the Jewish followers of Jesus in Judea, Israel, and Syria. Long before his vision on the Damascus Road, part of Paul was a sensitive human being with close ties to his extended family.

Knowing about his relationship with his two cousins and his nephew, we can more easily understand how deeply Paul was connected to them. Now we better understand the impact of those words to him on the Damascus Road. His two cousins give us a deeper insight into those words discussed earlier: "It is hard for you to kick against the goads [of your conscience]." It was not only blindness that struck Paul on that road; it was his sensitive heart. If his heart had been fully hardened, he might have simply continued on his violent, compulsive persecution of Jewish Christians.

People raised in nuclear families in the Western world too often miss the import of these interpersonal family connections when they read the Jewish and Christian scriptures. They do not understand the present bonding of Jewish families and many other family systems around the world. Jewish families still tend to bond quite closely both then and now in Israel. We unconsciously impose our own scattered Western nuclear family mentality when we read the scriptures.

In my own nuclear family, we would visit my aunt and uncle who lived over one hundred miles away about twice a year. My family lived in a national forest, and they lived in a very crowded metropolis, yet my aunt and uncle and my cousins Joe and Mary, who were almost my same age, had an indelible effect on my own values and life.

My cousin Mary enjoyed swimming, and she encouraged me to get over my fear of water. Thus, I eventually learned how to swim, dive, and surf the waves. My cousin Joe ran a high school mile just over four minutes, and he encouraged me to become more athletic. I am grateful to both of my cousins for their examples.

Paul's cousins also had to have had a significant effect on his life. Unmarried men like Paul emotionally rely on their extended families because they have no spouse or children. Paul's cousins realized Jesus was the Messiah before Paul did. Paul had to have had a lot of repressed emotions on his anti-Christian crusade, but the dam of those emotions broke on the Damascus Road.

Like you and me, as we think about Paul's stubbornness, we realize that we too have more than once resisted the quiet directions of God's still voice to our hearts. We too have dampened the dictates of our own conscience. We also have been at times stubborn to the point of denial. We all are like Paul of Tarsus. I'm sure this is why Paul has agitated me for the past sixty years. My own resistance to God and to good, like Paul's, is one of the reasons you are reading these words right now. Indeed, we are all too often like Paul of Tarsus, and so we desperately need to follow his consistent theme which *is all about Jesus.*

CHAPTER 16

Religious Structure Can Bind and Ease a Person's Anxiety

Why do so many Christians make Jesus and the four gospels postscripts to Paul's epistles? Why do they allow Paul's words to overshadow the words and life of Jesus? Repeatedly, Paul has said that he is simply laying the "foundation" for the church. He is only a faithful servant of Jesus of Nazareth. What is going on?

One answer to this phenomenon is the psychological reality we discussed earlier. The more anxious we are, the more structure we need to feel safe. Paul felt safe using the Torah, the Hebrew prophets, the Psalms, the detailed laws in the book of Leviticus, the Ten Commandments, and a total of 613 different Jewish laws that gradually developed over hundreds of years of Judaism. This structure at first made Paul feel safe. Later, he consistently decried them and said that coming to God was not about works and good deeds but all about "grace" and "faith" from the understanding of God through Jesus of Nazareth.

As I was writing this book, I was talking with two retired psychiatrist friends, one Roman Catholic and the other Jewish. We were discussing how indeed we lived in a world of multidimensional anxiety, and one of them said, "Who isn't anxious today?" We all smiled. With instant internet, cell phones, and news communications around the planet, every human being tends to be more anxious than our ancestors were. No wonder religions with too-easy answers flourish in the twenty-first century.

CHAPTER 17

Islam's Structure Makes a Person Feel Safe Like Paul

In 1980, I presented an eight-week series on Islam and Christianity. It was long before there was any mosque in Topeka, the center of the Bible belt. I knew that black Muslims would attend because it was advertised in the newspapers. The black Muslims did show up and were very polite when they realized this was not a polemic against them but an honest comparison between Islam and the Christian faith. When the church was packed for eight weeks with others, I realized something else was going on. I began to inquire.

I asked several visitors what drew them to the lectures. Several persons who were former Lutherans and Roman Catholics had quietly converted to Islam and wanted to be informed about Christianity and Islam by the lectures. Then I began to ask myself, *Why would they want to do that?* I realized that first, Lutherans and Catholics had rather strict catechisms and belief systems. They already had a lot of religious structure. It made them feel safe. Second, Islam provides even more structure and more freedom from anxiety.

Then I had an insight into Paul. Islam had even more structures than the Lutheran and the Roman Catholic faiths. When you have a strong structure, you don't have to think. Serious thinking can cause a lot of anxiety. It is easier to obey rules than to ponder religious things. This same reality applies to certain Christian groups, atheists, and also other extremists. It was safer emotionally living in "group think" than to individually struggle with complex spiritual issues. This structure can free some people from a lot of anxiety. This false sense of freedom leads to a false life.

CHAPTER 18

Paul's Lists of Dos and Don'ts

In his epistles, Paul of Tarsus has several lists of dos and don'ts. Every one of his epistles contains significant structure because after all, he was building the foundation of the church. He was setting up a new system. He has rules for "apostles, prophets, evangelists, pastors, and teachers." He lists rules for women, Communion, elders, deacons, ministering to widows, helping the hungry, and orphans. These rules have helped the church exist for over two thousand years. They are concrete rules. They make a person feel safe.

Jesus's teachings are more global and ultimately more demanding than the needed structure Paul provided. Jesus was right brained (Aramaic) and thus emotive. Jesus spoke in a holistic manner. Paul's rules are simple and concrete. Jesus spoke from his right brain. Paul was emotional too, but he spoke from his left brain. Western culture is left brain. Eastern culture is right brain.

Greek and Roman languages and culture are concrete and left brain. They are logical. They are sequential. Aramaic, Hebrew, Arabic, and Asian languages tend to be right brain, global, and more powerful emotionally. Following Jesus's words and life is hard work. Understanding the nuances of his life and teachings demands total commitment. Peace cannot be attained part-time.

His words make a person think and live deeply: body, soul, mind, and spirit. Christianity would not exist without the practical and logical foundation Paul has laid. Paul was indeed a great apostle, but rules demand only obedience. Jesus demands heart and soul.

Far too many Christians live out their faith based on legalism. Too often, they change Paul's teachings into additional rules and regulations. It is most important to live out a life of emotional and magnanimous giving and the unconditional love of Jesus of Nazareth. It is also more difficult than legalistic rules. *It is all about Jesus.*

CHAPTER 19

Similarities between Paul's Life and That of the Prophet Jonah

Paul's life was similar to the Prophet Jonah's. As we think about Paul and Jonah in this chapter, we need to remember that we are Jonah too, just like Paul. Jonah's mission was to liberate Nineveh and give the non-Jewish Hittites God's message so that they could repent. Jonah tried to sail away, far from Nineveh, to the far side of the world to what is now known as the Iberian Peninsula or Spain. The Hittites were not Jews and were enemies.

Jonah found he could never get beyond God's reach. His hatred for the Hittites was so intense that he disobeyed God even though his calling was to be a prophet of God. Like Jonah, Paul found on the road to Damascus that he could never get beyond God's reach.

The Hittites were enemies of Israel. They were not the chosen Jewish people. Jonah did not want them to repent. Nonetheless, he was forced to become obedient to God. The book of Jonah records that in spite of his initial unwillingness to obey God, Jonah fulfilled his mission in life. When Nineveh repented in sackcloth and ashes from the king down to the common citizen, Jonah was greatly upset. He did not want non-Jews to become believers in his Most High God.

Jewish Christians were seen by Paul as enemies of Israel and of the Hebrew faith. They acted like the chosen people. Paul's obedience to God and the dramatic reframing of his mission in life are a major turning point in world history and culture. We are all God's children. When Paul became a follower of Jesus, his life had a paradigm shift. From persecuting Christian Jews, he took an even deeper step like Jonah did. He was commissioned by God to take the Good News of Jesus of Nazareth both to Jews and non-Jews alike. The apostle Paul's life does indeed parallel the life of the prophet Jonah. Paul could not run from his conscience. Neither can we.

CHAPTER 20

Paul's Religious Addiction Was Like the Gerasene Demoniac

During half a century as an ordained Christian minister, as a US Army chaplain, and as a licensed clinical addiction counselor, I have encountered darkness in the lives of many in clinics, mental hospitals, military units, and churches. Darkness, not surprisingly, co-occurs in people with numerous types of addictions. Religious addiction is quite often comorbid with the darkness of behavioral addictions or the darkness of chemical addictions. Over the years, religious addiction became increasingly a concrete fact to me. It is just as dark if not darker.

All addictions are deadly mental health disorders. The religious addict's misunderstandings about God can become as terminal as any addiction, such as a gambling addiction, and as deadly as any drink or any legal or illegal drug. Father Leo Booth was a pioneer in this field of understanding and wrote some foundational books on this reality. Religious addiction, since it can be just as obsessive and compulsive, is quite dangerous in its own right.

The naked, "demon-possessed" madman in the Gerasene cemetery had been out of control for a long time, yet he ran and "bowed in worship" at Jesus's feet. The demons did not want to come out of this man, but at Jesus's command, they had to leave. Even though he was under the control of a "mob" of demons, the man was able to run and kneel at Jesus's feet and "worship" him.

When Jesus drove the mob of demons out of him, the Gerasene man's right mind came back to him and he allowed Jesus's followers to cover his nakedness with clothing. When others from the non-Jewish area of the "Ten Towns" (only non-Jews would raise pigs) came to see what had happened to him, they were amazed. They saw the former deranged man "sitting there decently clothed and making sense." The man's right mind had come back to him. Paul's right mind also came back to him after he heard the voice, saw the light, and had Ananias explain to him Jesus's call on his life and pray for his sight to return.

The man begged Jesus to let him become one of his followers and go with him, but Jesus said, "Go home to your people and tell them your story ... The man went back and began to proclaim in all of the Ten Towns what Jesus had done for him. He was the talk of the town" (Mark 5:20 MSG). Paul went to every corner of the world he could reach, telling about the light and love of Jesus of Nazareth, just as the demoniac did in that Ten Town Gentile area.

It is certain that many of the Greeks, Romans, and others in that area where the formerly demon-possessed person lived later became followers of Jesus because of that man's personal testimony. The man whom Jesus had set free wanted to follow him, but Jesus told him to stay and tell what "great things God had done" for him. He obeyed and fulfilled his mission in life.

Paul's religious addiction was more cognitive than the demoniac's but still strikingly like this crazed, Gerasene madman before he was set free and became a follower of Jesus of Nazareth. Paul was truly addicted to religion because he had stood by while Stephan was stoned to death, and then he congratulated murderers.

Paul's deadly addiction to right-wing Judaism made him just as crazy as the madman. Paul was ready to kill and imprison to support his understanding of Judaism by violence. Terrorists of all faith groups who have this religiously addictive stance believe with blind simplicity that the end justifies the means. It may seem shocking to some of you reading these words to think of Paul as a religious terrorist or as a man possessed by demons. Religious addiction indeed can be more than shocking.

There were other Jewish leaders at that time, some quietly and some openly, who were becoming followers of the Nazarene.

Paul had heard stories about Jesus's teachings, miracles, and healings, but like many other Jews of his age, he had rejected the stories because Jesus did not meet his criteria for a Messiah. He wanted an earthly king who would drive the Romans out of Judea. If you and I were Jews in Paul's time, we might also have wanted the same type of Messiah.

On the road to Damascus, his religious addiction to Judaism was knocked out of him. He was humbled. When God spoke to Paul through one of Jesus's followers, Ananias, he was healed. His blindness, his insane, obsessive-compulsive (and one could say demonic) addictive religious disorder also went away. Paul went on and fulfilled his divine mission in life. The demon of religious addiction had permanently left Paul. Now his life would be totally dedicated to the One who restored his sight, Jesus of Nazareth, his Messiah. *Paul was all about Jesus.*

CHAPTER 21

Paul from Jonathan Sack's Book, Not in God's Name

When religion turns men into murderers, God weeps. Having made human beings in his image, God sees the first man and woman disobey the first command, and the first human child commits the murder. Within a short space of time, "the world was filled with violence" … too often in the history of religion, people have killed in the name of God, waged war in the name of the God of peace, hated in the name of the God of love, and practiced cruelty in the name of the God of compassion. (3)

Saul's early life clearly followed this murderous, violent path, but after the Damascus Road, the tables turned the opposite way. Then it was Paul who was the hated one and who was attacked, stoned, cruelly treated, and sentenced to death by religious leaders who had Nero in Rome carry out Paul's violent death on a cross. It is so important to realize it was not the

Jewish people themselves. Every intelligent, informed Jew at the time knew beyond a doubt that Jesus was a great prophet.

I want to restate how very important it is to realize that the Jewish people as a whole knew that Jesus was a great prophet on the magnitude of Moses or Elijah. Their religious leaders, however, were afraid that Jesus's incredible popularity would destabilize Judea, forcing the Romans to come in with all their military might. The Sadducees, to be even more specific, were terrified of losing their political power.

The Sadducees in charge of the temple were the spiritual descendants of Judas Maccabaeus. The Sadducees ran the temple complex, the animal sacrifices, and the money changers. Judas Maccabaeus, his brothers, and the Judean people had overthrown the Greeks and driven them out of Judea. This took place almost two hundred years before the Romans came on the scene.

The Sadducees were in charge of the religious body known as the High Priesthood. They had been in power for a long time, ever since the Maccabean Revolt. They were entrenched in power. They loved power. Jesus directly criticized their lust for power, and they hated him and had been waiting for many months to kill him. When Rome destroyed Jerusalem in approximately 70 CE, the Sadducees ceased to exist. Judaism itself continued onward for centuries to our present age because it has so much more emotional and spiritual substance.

CHAPTER 22

Pathological Dualism and Paul of Tarsus

Sack talks about what he calls

> pathological dualism that sees humanity itself
> as radically, ontologically divided into the
> unimpeachably good and the irredeemably bad.
> You are either one or the other: either one of the
> saved the redeemed, the chosen, or a child of
> Satan, the devil's disciple. (51)

Extreme religions of all types: Islam, Hinduism, Christianity, and others suffer from this pathology as well. It is unfortunate that many of those who sing the praises of Paul of Tarsus and quote him more than they quote the loving words of Jesus of Nazareth can sometimes exhibit the same "pathological dualism" of which Sacks speaks.

They tend to see truth as totally right or totally wrong with no middle ground. Both extreme liberals and extreme conservatives tend to be this way. Both sides think about "burning people at the stake" who disagree with them. Both sides can call people who disagree with them "demon possessed" or ignorant and uneducated over fairly minor issues.

CHAPTER 23

A Personal Example of Extreme Right or Wrong Thinking

I was studying the original koine Greek of the Christian scriptures in the New Testament and was beginning to realize that the word Jesus used to describe wine always meant alcoholic wine. Another student, Reuben Sequira, also in the graduate school of theology we both attended strongly disagreed with me and vigorously stated that the Greek word for *wine* had to be "freshly squeezed grape juice." We had quite an argument.

Dr. J. Harold Greenlee was walking down the hallway when we were loudly and animatedly arguing. Dr. Greenlee was one of the leading Greek scholars in the United States at that time. I asked Dr. Greenlee about this as he walked by, and he replied, "That word always means alcoholic wine."

Reuben responded, "I don't care what it means; it was freshly squeezed grape juice." Subsequently, I actually heard this same graduate student call others "demon possessed" when they disagreed with him on other theological points. What an unmistakable example of pathological dualism, religious addiction, and a cruel, unthinking, hardened, inflexible belief system.

CHAPTER 24

The Pathological Dualism of Zoroaster

Sack describes a modern example of "pathological dualism" as exhibited by some of the leaders of Shiite Islam. Zoroaster, mentioned in detail in the next chapter in this book, was a great prophet who was a precursor of even the Hebrew prophets. He was born in 628 BCE in Persia in what is now known as Iran.

Zoroaster saw all theological issues starkly in black and white, right and wrong. Truth was absolute. Shiite Islam in Persia inculcated this simplistic mentality into their version of Islam.

No wonder Persian religious leaders to this day blatantly call Russians, Americans, or anyone with whom they disagree "the Great Satan."

Sack continues,

> Paul is one of the most complex figures in the history of religion. Thousands of books have been written about him, and there are major differences of opinion about his personality, his

> theology, and especially his relationship with
> Jews and Judaism. (92)

Paul's apparent dualism was also linked to the prophet Zoroaster's initial thoughts.

CHAPTER 25

Zoroastrian Influence on the Hebrew Prophets and Paul

Everyone is in part a child of the age in which he or she lives, and Paul was no exception. During the Babylonian Captivity of the Jewish people, their thinking was radically altered by the teachings of Zoroaster.

Zoroastrianism is one of the world's religions with the longest continuity. It greatly declined after the Islamic faith reached Persia in 650 CE but still exists today. It is a monotheistic faith that teaches about the struggles between right and wrong, light and darkness, with the good overcoming evil in the end. Zoroastrian thought shaped the Persian Empire and thus greatly influenced Judaism and later Christianity and Islam.

Zoroaster taught that everyone is free to decide either for the light or for the darkness. Zoroastrians believe that at death, the body is evil, unlike most Jews or Christians. They build towers so these evil bodies will be eaten by vultures. Zoroaster called God's name, Ahura Mazda, and said he was a "wise" God.

Many scholars believe that the "Wise Men" from Persia were Zoroastrian priests who saw the star mentioned in the Christian scriptures and came to worship Jesus as a child in Bethlehem. Thus, the Pharisaical faith of Paul of Tarsus had a tendency to view things as either right or wrong, and this was a part of Paul's lifelong stance. To a degree, Paul's mentor was Zoroaster.

First, Paul persecuted Jewish Christians. Later, his ministry was rescuing Gentiles and Jews from the darkness of life without Jesus into the light of God's love, forgiveness, and grace. The light on the Damascus Road confirmed this concept to Paul. It was the final, absolute proof he was coming out of the darkness into the light of God's wise and loving direction in his life.

CHAPTER 26

Peter's Three Visions that Gentiles Were Now Equal to Jews

Paul had a huge paradigm shift, for a person who had been born and raised as a Jew, when he agreed with Peter and the early Jewish church in Jerusalem that no human being was unclean. Paul followed Peter's lead that "salvation" was for everyone and not primarily for the Jews. Ananias's words that he was being sent to the Gentiles and Jews had to also have greatly affected Paul.

Before Paul's conversion, Saint Peter had the very same difficulty. Then Peter in three visions experienced three repeated commands to "take and eat" food that used to be unclean. Peter began to see that no one was unclean and that Jesus was for every person on the planet.

Later, Paul, with the apostle Peter's forceful support and help, had the difficult task of changing the Jewish mind-set of the early Jerusalem church in accepting "outsiders" as full-fledged followers of Jesus. Later, the social pressure of Jewish Christians in Jerusalem caused Peter to temporarily recant back into Judaism and forget his visions.

Paul then had to forcefully remind Peter of his threefold vision that Gentiles were no longer outcasts from the Good News that Jesus was the Messiah. Then Paul and Peter together taught the Jewish believers in Jerusalem and Judea that these "God-fearers" who were Greeks and non-Jews were also entitled to become part of the newly forming fellowship of the followers of Jesus.

CHAPTER 27

Locations of Many Christian Worship Centers

Interestingly, the first Christian church buildings in the Roman world were often located close to the Jewish synagogues where the first Jewish and Gentile Christian converts were made. Over time, these God-fearers and Christian Jews gradually developed the belief system that all Christians were also the children of the house of Jacob, spiritual followers, and full heirs of Isaac. This was naturally grating on the ears of those who still followed Judaism.

This activity happened almost within earshot of the synagogues. That would be stressful for any established religious group. Not only were many Jews and non-Jews recruited by Paul into following Jesus, they also worshipped next door or within a short distance of the synagogue. It was a socially incendiary powder keg in many large cities.

Unfortunately, some of new Gentile Christians began to believe and teach that biological Jews were more like the children of Ishmael, the banished firstborn son, and the ill-conceived eldest son of Isaac. This judgmental attitude served neither Christians nor Jews very well in Paul's time though it continues clear into our present age.

Paul had a problem, because he was banding together the biological Jews who were followers of Jesus and the non-Jewish followers of Jesus. He taught them they were both equal partners in the kingdom of God.

It was difficult for many Jewish believers, some of whom were still practicing Jews, to make this shift in their thinking. Shortly before his final arrest and voyage to Rome, Paul also appeared to have had some of his ambiguity about the early church's Jewish roots and his own Jewish heritage, because he did a Jewish ritual cleansing rite at the temple in Jerusalem.

He and four other Jewish men, as reported in Acts 21, had taken a vow during the "days of purification." They had shaved their heads and were preparing to give the purification "offering." Jews from Ephesus saw him doing this in the temple in Jerusalem.

These Jews from Ephesus may very well have been part of the huge riot in that city on Paul's missionary journey there. These men attacked Paul, dragged him out of the temple, and were preparing to kill him when the commanding tribune of the Roman Army heard about the turmoil. He immediately took his soldiers and saved Paul from being murdered.

Paul was in a difficult emotional and cultural spot on this issue. His faith now made him neither Jew nor Gentile. He too was still in the process of having his cultural roots bent and broken by Jesus's life, words, and sacrifice on the cross. I'm sure he remembered Ananias's prophetic words that he would learn to know the emotional "pain" of his new missionary task.

CHAPTER 28

Jews Are "Disinherited, Violated, and Robbed"

Reading Paul's letters in the Christian scriptures tends to make many Jews feel that they have been "disinherited, violated, and robbed of an identity" (Sacks, 96). According to Paul's writings, Christians were now the Children of Israel.

"Paul in the epistle to the Romans, performs a second reversal, arguing that it is the younger religion, Christianity, which has replaced the elder, Judaism, as heir to the covenant." Sacks goes on to say that exactly the same reversal happened in Islam in rejecting both Christianity and Judaism (109).

There has always been anti-Semitism from the beginning: Egyptians, Amalekites, Edomites, Philistines, and the Assyrians, where the book of Esther so accurately and historically testifies to the livid details of anti-Semitism.

Sack believes that in the third century, Cyprian continued this core of anti-Semitism, which grew under the teachings of the church fathers Tertullian, John Chrysostom, and Aphrahat. Later, there were numerous pogroms against the European Jews, three hundred years of Crusades against Jews and followers of Islam, and forced expulsions of Jews from England in 1290 and from Spain in 1492 (see Addendum 3 regarding the emigration of Jews from Spain to Sarajevo).

Martin Luther repeatedly uttered incredible anti-Jewish polemical statements (read about Martin Luther later in this book). This was due in part to Luther's consistent focus on Paul's writings. Luther read anti-Semitism into the writings of Paul's epistles. Paul was writing about specific, infuriated Jews who attacked him. Paul was not writing about Jews in general.

Luther's errors about the Jews being "Christ-killers" and later centuries of reproach culminated in over six million Jews dying in the death camps of Hitler. Thus, it became a necessity for the survival of the world population of Jewish peoples that the formation of the State of Israel took place on May 14, 1948. Sacks calls this process *the revenge of the rejected*.

Several books have addressed the psychological struggles of Paul. "He wrestled long and hard with the phenomenon of guilt" (Sacks, 153). I think it is very interesting that after counseling patients of all faith groups and specifically Christians for over fifty years, I have found that those who espoused Paul's teachings the most intensely also suffered guilt and shame issues much more than the average person who walks in the door of my clinic, Hope for Life.

Paul's teachings are misread by many people, and in my opinion, this misreading of Paul's words and thoughts have significantly contributed to the self-shame and self-guilt of far too many Christians. Shame and guilt were not the stances of the Jesus of Nazareth whose life categorically said, "Neither do I condemn you. Go and sin no more" (John 8:11).

CHAPTER 29

Richard Rohr and the Struggle between "Flesh" and "Ego"

Theologian N. T. Wright teaches that Paul's major theme is *the new temple of God is the human person.* Paul's thought is that being in such a position "brings a deep new sense of the inherent dignity of every human person." Over time, this came to mean, in part, the French Enlightenment's understanding in the Constitution of the United States that every person has basic human rights.

These constitutional statements of human rights are based on Paul's understanding that human beings who follow Jesus are the temple of God. One core value of democracies in the West is the value of each person. Valuing human beings is not seen in the dictatorships of the world. This is blatantly apparent in the histories of Germany, China, and Russia. Paul authenticates Jesus's concern for every human being and is to be commended for doing so. In far too many societies on this planet, human beings are seen as expendable and of little individual worth.

Richard Rohr[1] says, "Paul is forever the critic of immature, self-serving religion, and the pioneer of mature and truly life-changing religion." Rohr continues, "The problem is not between body and spirit; it's between part and whole. Every time Paul uses the word *flesh*, just replace it with the word *ego*, and you will be much closer to his point."

"After conversion, God is not 'out there.' You are in God and God is in you. Believers exist as parts of the whole, the Body of Christ. Their very existence is the shared state that Paul calls 'love' or living 'in Christ."

Philippians is Richard Rohr's

> favorite of Paul's letters because it describes how we need to work with the rebellious, angry, and dualistic mind. Paul wrote his letter to the Philippians during one of his many imprisonments. He even mentioned being in chains, and yet ironically this is the most positive and joy-filled of all of his letters.

In a most succinct and perfect summary, Paul says that you should "Pray with gratitude, and the peace of God which is beyond all knowledge, will guard your hearts and your minds in Christ Jesus" (Philippians 4:6–7 MSG).

---

[1] Material adapted from Richard Rohr's words by the Center for Action and Contemplation, *In the Footsteps of St. Paul* (Franciscan Media, 2015).

"First, you must *begin with the positive*, with gratitude (which might take your whole prayer time). Second, you need to *pray as long it takes you to find "peace,"* to get to a place beyond agitation (whether five minutes or five hours or five days). Third, note that Rohr says this is a place beyond "knowledge," beyond processing information or ideas. Fourth, you must learn how to *stand guard*, which is what many call "creating the inner witness" or the witnessing presence that calmly watches your flow of thoughts (mind) and feelings (heart).

> Finally, you must know what the goal is: your egotistical thoughts can actually be replaced with living inside the very mind of Christ (*en Christo*). This is not self-generated knowing, but knowing by participation—consciousness itself (*con-scire*, to know with).

Paul then goes on to suggest that we fill our minds "with everything that is true, everything that is noble, everything that is good, everything that we love and honor, everything that can be thought virtuous or worthy of praise" (Philippians 4:8 MSG). Norman Vincent Peale called this "the power of positive thinking." I call it "replacement therapy."

> If we don't choose love and compassion, the human mind naturally goes in the other direction, and we risk joining a vast majority of people who live their later years trapped in a sense of victimhood, entitlement, and bitterness. We

are not free until we are free from our own compulsiveness, our own resentments, our own complaining, and our own obsessive patterns of thinking.

We have to catch these patterns early in their development and nip them in the bud. And where's the bud? It's in the mind. That's the primary place where we sin, as Jesus himself says (Matthew 5:21–48). Any later behaviors are just a response to the way our minds work. We can't walk around all day writing negative, hateful mental commentaries about other people, or we will become hate itself.

CHAPTER 30

The Relationship between Law and Grace

The Relationship between Law and Grace (Rohr Continues)[2]

Almost anyone involved in their Christian faith has experienced this struggle. Basically, it is the creative tension between religion as requirements and religion as transformation. Is God's favor based on a performance principle (Law)? Or does religion work within an entirely different economy and equation?

This is a necessary boxing match, but a match in which grace must win. When it doesn't, religion becomes moralistic, which is merely the ego's need for order and control. I am sorry to say, but this is most garden-variety religion. We must recover grace-oriented spirituality if we are to rebuild Christianity from the bottom up.

---

[2] Material adapted from Richard Rohr (*Things Hidden: Scripture as Spirituality* [Franciscan Media, 2008], 72, 78–79, 82.

In Romans and Galatians, Paul gives us sophisticated studies of the meaning, purpose, and limitations of law. He says its function is just to get us started, but legalism too often takes over. Yet Paul's brilliant analysis has had little effect on the continued Christian idealization of law, even though he makes it very clear: Laws can only give us information; they cannot give us transformation (Romans 3:20; 7:7–13).

Laws can give us very good boundaries, but boundary-keeping of itself is a long way from love.

Many people and contemporary attorneys at law in Western civilization may not be aware of the very complicated legal terms Paul uses in his writings. As the United States was growing westward in its second great expansion, newly founded law schools would often study the legal arguments of Paul, particularly in the book of Romans, as teaching texts for US common law legal arguments.

Paul describes Israel as looking for a righteousness derived from the law and yet failing to achieve the purposes of the law. Why did they fail? Because they relied on being privately good instead of trusting in God for their goodness! In other words, they stumbled over the stumbling stone (see Romans 9:31–32).

Law is a necessary stage, but if we stay there, Paul believes, it actually becomes a major obstacle to transformation into love and mercy.

Law often frustrates the process of transformation by becoming an end in itself. It inoculates us from the real thing, which is always relationship. Paul says that God gave us the law to show us that we can't obey the law! (See Romans 7:7–13 if you don't believe me.) Paul even says that the written law brings death, and only the Spirit can bring life (Romans 7:5–6; 2 Corinthians 3:6). This man is truly radical, but it did not take churches long to domesticate him. We've treated Paul as if he were a moralist instead of the first-rate mystic and teacher that he is.

Ironically, until people have had some level of inner God experience, there is no point in asking them to follow Jesus' ethical ideals. It is largely a waste of time. Indeed, they will not be able to even understand the law's meaning and purpose. Religious requirements only become the source of deeper anxiety.

Humans quite simply don't have the power to obey any spiritual law, especially issues like forgiveness of enemies, nonviolence, self-emptying, humble use of power, true justice toward the outsider ... except in and through union with God. Or as Jesus put it, "the branch cut off from the vine is useless" (John 15:5).

CHAPTER 31

The Wise Words of an Elderly Minister to Focus on Jesus

I was attending a spiritual retreat at King Solomon Camp in Solomon, Kansas. This retreat was put on by the independent Christian Churches of Kansas. They are a very conservative branch of the American religious movement that followed the leadership of Alexander Campbell. They are one of the few homegrown faith groups in the United States. Campbell believed that all Christians who follow Jesus were brothers and sisters and not only deserved Holy Communion but equal respect regardless of their secondary understandings of things like modes of baptism and so on. Independent Christians tend to believe that every single word of the Christian scriptures are equally inspired by God. They put Jesus's words and Paul's words on the same level.

Therefore, there is no distinction between the life and teachings of Jesus and the life and teachings of Paul in the Christian scriptures or New Testament. They generally regard Paul as speaking ex cathedra for Jesus.

If you listen closely to their words, Jesus's life and teachings are more often described in the words, thoughts, and understanding of Paul rather than viewing them through the other teachings, life, and actions of Jesus in the gospels. I therefore was both surprised and delighted to hear David J. Pape, the beloved retired pastor of University Christian Church in Manhattan, Kansas, echo one of the main themes of this book. With his expressed permission, I quote verbatim his scripture and his spoken words[3]:

> *You are blessed when you care. At the moment of being "care-full," you find yourselves cared for. You are blessed when you get your inside world—your mind and heart—put right. Then you see God in the outside world. You are blessed when you can show people how to cooperate instead of compete or fight. That's when you discover who you really are and your place in God's family. You are blessed when your commitment to God provokes persecution. The persecution drives you even deeper into God's kingdom.*
>
> *Not only that—count yourselves blessed every time people put you down or throw you out or speak lies about you to discredit me. What it means is that the truth is too close for comfort*

---

[3] Used with direct permission.

> *and they are uncomfortable. You can be glad when that happens—give a cheer, even!—For though you don't like it, I do! And all heaven applauds. And know that you are in good company. My prophets and witnesses have always gotten into this kind of trouble (Matthew 5:7–12 MSG).*

Then Rev. Pape shared a key spiritual insight he had gained over the years.

> I have an increasing appreciation for the teachings of Jesus. I don't think I gave them as much weight in my early years of preaching as I would give them today. I kind of picked this up from some of my college classes. I got the idea that because Jesus taught before the cross then we would give more emphasis to the Book of Acts and the Letters (primarily of Paul) and not focus as much in the church on the teachings of Jesus in the Gospels.

> I think now that this was not the most spiritually healthy thing that I could have done for myself. After all, if Jesus was God, it doesn't make any difference when he was talking. It is to my own good that I would listen closely to what he says.

The thing about Jesus's teachings is that they keep me balanced. 1. When I start getting proud, his words show me my own sin. 2. When I get judgmental, he reminds me that only God can judge. 3. When I start getting narrow, his words remind me of how broad God's grace is. 4. He won't let me be satisfied. His words make me spiritually hungry. 5. He won't let me get too discouraged. His words remind me of our eternal hope. 6. He will not let me faint and fall under my sin. He reminds me that he has carried that sin for me. And so more and more I find myself being refreshed by the words of Jesus.

As a boy I was fortunate to hear the Gospels (not the Epistles of Paul) read by my father for a morning devotion. My dad died when I had just turned 11, but at ages 8, 9, and 10 I remember him calling us all into the living room with mom. There were 12 of us kids then. My baby sister had been born a couple of weeks after his funeral to make 13, but dad would call us all in and read a chapter from the Bible, often from the Sermon on the Mount and he would pray and we would say the Lord's Prayer together. You are familiar with the book, "All I ever needed to know I learned in Kindergarten?" Maybe that is why I have found renewal and refreshing in the teachings of Jesus. I'm going back to the roots of my faith.

I have an increasing appreciation for the teachings of Jesus.

CHAPTER 32

Franciscans Modeled Their Lives on Jesus and Not Solely on Paul

I was amazed to learn in Sarajevo that one of the first governmental decrees for religious toleration in world history was made by the Ottoman Turks when they saw how much like Jesus the priests and monks of the Franciscan order were treating Roman Catholics, Orthodox believers, the followers of Islam, and everyone else.

Many scholars of history believe that St. Francis was more like Jesus of Nazareth than almost any other person in world history, and I strongly agree. St. Francis and his Jesus-centered theology renewed the church from one thousand years of decline. It was the Franciscans and their Jesus-of-Nazareth-like behaviors that caused the fierce Islamic Ottoman Turks to honor them by not driving them out of Sarajevo and the Ottoman Empire like they did all the other Christian groups.

The Roman Catholic Church was in a low moral and ethical state when St. Francis arrived on the scene in Rome to ask for his followers to become a new monastic order. Francis was more focused than the other orders on following Jesus's command for chastity, fidelity, and poverty exactly as Jesus had commanded. The Franciscans left every personal tie, property, and possession—every single thing—to be totally dedicated to Jesus's lifestyle and message.

At first, the local bishops and priests saw the Franciscans as threats to their parishes, but over time, the sunny, positive, nonthreatening, Jesus-like monks and priests of the Franciscans made their own statement by the actions of their lives. The Ottoman Turks in Sarajevo saw precisely the same reflection of Jesus five hundred years after the Franciscan order was founded. To this day, the Franciscans and the Capuchins are all about Jesus. My most admired Catholic saint is Padre Pio, an incredibly gifted monk in the early twentieth century, who was born in an obscure region of the boot heel of Italy. Pio was also *all about Jesus.*

CHAPTER 33

Personal Words on the Franciscans and Jesus and Paul

I grew up knowing the history of the Franciscan missionaries who sacrificed their lives to bring the Chumash Indians and other Native Americans a faith in a loving God along the one-thousand-mile coast from Baja California to Northern California.

When I attended Mass to work on my Latin skills in high school in the old Franciscan-constructed Queen of the Missions Church in Santa Barbara, I did my own research on Padre Junipero Serra and all the Franciscans. Padre Serra and those who followed him stood up to Spanish merchants, adventurers, and even soldiers who wanted to exploit the Native Americans, whom the Franciscans tried to protect. To the faithful Franciscans' sorrow, a huge percentage of the natives who came in contact with the Europeans died of smallpox, measles, viruses, and the flu inadvertently brought into California by the European Spaniards.

To this day, the Franciscans still remain in California and in Sarajevo, Tuzla, and in other parts of the former Ottoman Empire, in spite of the areas being under the control of Islamic politicians for five centuries. It was a direct result of their selfless service to doing good deeds to all people. To the Franciscans, it was all about Jesus.

Had the Franciscans modeled their lives not on Jesus but rather on the teachings of Paul, who had a starker, more legalistic approach to the faith, it would not have worked out well. The Islamic Ottoman Empire's reprieve would never have taken place, and the Franciscans' wonderful ministries to the California Native Americans would never have occurred.

The Franciscan Monk, Richard Rohr, mentioned earlier, points out the difference between orthodoxy, which is about obedience, and orthopraxy, which is endeavoring to be like Jesus.

> By emphasizing practice over theory, or orthopraxy over orthodoxy, the Franciscan tradition taught that love and action are more important than intellect or speculative truth ... Orthodoxy teaches us the theoretical importance of love; orthopraxy helps us learn how to love, which is much more difficult. To be honest, even my Franciscan seminary training was far better at teaching me how to obey and conform than

how to love. I'm still trying to learn how to love every day of my life.

As we endeavor to put love into action, we come to realize that, on our own, we are unable to obey Jesus' command to "Love one another as I have loved you." To love as Jesus loves, we must be connected to the Source of love.

Franciscan life teaches that connection in solitude, silence, and some form of contemplative prayer, all of which quiet the monkey mind and teach us emotional sobriety and psychological freedom from our addictions and attachments. Otherwise, most talk of "repentance" or "change of life" is largely an illusion and pretense.

As a Christian Church (Disciples of Christ) pastor, my first spiritual director was Sister Barbara of Sisters of St. Francis of the Holy Eucharist Convent, in Independence, Missouri. She led me and a group of other seekers each week in their chapel teaching *Lectio Divina*, which focuses on letting the scriptures deeply sink into one's soul.

It was not by chance that in this same Franciscan convent, the Christian Church of Greater Kansas City sponsored a retreat for Disciples of Christ clergy with Father Thomas Keating, early advocate of centering prayer, in the mid-1980s. Centering prayer, in the presence of Jesus of Nazareth, dramatically changed my life forever. *It is all about Jesus.*

CHAPTER 34

Paul, the Storm, and the People of Malta

One has to have both an honest and a humble heart to accept the teachings of the life of Jesus of Nazareth. An honest and humble person is automatically a loving and caring person. All of the positive virtues in a person's life tend to go together. As part of the process of writing this book on Paul, Kathleen and I traveled to the Island of Malta.

Malta has always had a reputation for hospitality and kindness throughout recorded history. The ancient temples in Malta are some of the oldest places of worship in the entire world and go back beyond 3,500 BCE.

The Maltese people were hungering and searching for God long before Paul of Tarsus told them of Jesus of Nazareth. These Maltese stone places of worship were created before the Egyptian pyramids and even before Stonehenge. I could see in the central places of both temples how people would be able to worship within those rough walls.

When my wife and I toured these two ancient temples on Malta, I was increasingly impressed that even granted the primitive nature of the walls themselves, in the interior, more finished work still retained a notable aura and sense of sanctity and worship that went beyond ancient, artistic craftsmanship.

The Island of Malta stands in a strategic position in the center of the Mediterranean Sea and in the world, straddling Africa, Europe, and the Middle East, just as Israel is at the four corners of Asia, the Middle East, Europe, and Africa. Malta has a historic legacy of promoting peace. It has witnessed the domination of the Minoans, the Egyptians, the Phoenicians, the Greeks, the Carthaginians, the Romans, the Germans, the French, and the British.

In more recent times, it has served in an international peacemaking role as when President George W. Bush and Premier Gorbachev first established Perestroika or "openness" between the Soviet Union and the West. It also rained the entire time that peacemaking conference was in progress.

Valletta Harbor in northern Malta. This is the
harbor where the huge grain ship with Paul
was headed before it broke apart on the rocky
eastern coast because of the winter storm.

CHAPTER 35

The Winter Storms of Malta

Paul of Tarsus was well aware of the annual winter storms and the incredibly forceful winds that swept across the breadth of the Mediterranean Sea. He had grown up in Asia Minor in Tarsus right on that sea and had seen those storms firsthand.

My wife and I experienced heavy winds in a previous October in this same region. Our cruise ship was on its way from Ephesus to Corinth, and in the face of the heavy winds, the captain of the ship had to abandon the Corinth destination; find shelter on the leeward, southwestern side of the Greek peninsula; and travel to Olympia instead. I was surprised that a modern ocean liner had tourists navigating in such rough weather. Paul's ship also had sailing problems.

Paul and the ship's captain had their nautical advice overruled by the Roman centurion and his soldiers, who were guarding Paul. This was a huge grain ship carrying tons of grain to Rome. Luke says it had three hundred passengers and crew.

The immense size of the grain ship might have given the centurion a false sense of security. Good army officers listen to their sergeants and those around them, but this Roman officer was not humble and wise enough to do so, and the ship headed straight into disaster. Paul knew that gale-force winds awaited them so he prayed for the safety of everyone on the ship. The storm grew in force, the clouds lowered, and it became impossible to safely navigate.

The only thing the ship could do was ride before the gale. The sailors threw out the tons of grain they were carrying to Rome to lighten the ship. They threw out sea anchors to slow the ship down and to keep it headed away from the billowing waves.

The sailors began to test the depth of the water because they sensed they were approaching land. Their depth weights indicated that land was coming closer. The sailors tried to put down lifeboats and escape, but Paul saw what the sailors were doing.

Paul told the centurion that if the sailors escaped, everyone else would die. The lifeboats were then cut away from the ship. Paul got all three hundred of the crew, passengers, and soldiers together and told them before he prayed for their safety that an angel of God had appeared to him and said that not one life would be lost in the shipwreck.

Paul encouraged them to eat so they would have strength because the storm had such power that having regular meals had been impossible. The sailors did not recognize the eastern part of the Island of Malta because they were used to entering the large, beautiful ports on the north of the island. The ship hit the shore hard and immediately began to break apart.

This shipwreck happened in AD 60. In a Malta museum are two stone anchors from Paul's time that might very well be from this exact ship. When the ship broke apart, the kind people of Malta extended warm hospitality in the winter weather, helping to get Paul and all three hundred of the ship's passengers and soldiers to land safely. They built a big bonfire to warm them up and then began taking them into their own homes, where they would remain for three months during the rest of the winter. The governor of Malta, Publicus, took Paul to his own quarters in the middle of the island.

Every member of the crew, all the soldiers and the passengers, and later the Maltese heard of Paul's prophesy that as bad as things looked, they needed to go ahead and eat something before the ship fell apart. They all heard that God had spoken to Paul and said that no one on the ship would die when it hit landfall, and no one died. Paul's prophesy came true. All three hundred people lived.

Everyone therefore realized that Paul was a man of God and at the very least a prophet. Word of this miracle and answer to prayer continued to spread like wildfire among the few thousand people who then lived on the island.

Good news again spread when it was learned that Paul had prayed for Governor Publicus's father, who had been gravely ill, and he had been healed. Then for the next three months, most of the island's inhabitants indirectly learned about Paul and had a chance to personally hear Paul tell the Good News of Jesus of Nazareth and share many of Jesus's teachings, deeds, and words.

There is no question that Paul tried systematically to share the teachings of Jesus every day and in every single way that he could. Evangelism was Paul's nature. Throughout the history of Christianity, it is often the lowest, most humble, and most honest people who first begin to follow God, and this was true in Malta. A humble, honest prophet from Galilee named Jesus of Nazareth resounded within their own humble hearts.

Now the formerly proud and violent man named Paul of Tarsus, who had been humbled and made honest by his encounter on the road to Damascus, was making a difference in Malta. This same spiritual and social reality exists clear into the twenty-first century. As discussed earlier, humble and honest people always respond to God. These people are drawn by the honesty, radiance, and trustworthy and spiritual lives of those like Paul. It was not by chance that Jesus was raised in the humble village of Nazareth. It was not by chance that Paul of Tarsus was shipwrecked on Malta.

CHAPTER 36

Paul, the Maltese Flag ... An Amazing Story of Maltese Faith

On the Island of Malta, where Paul of Tarsus was shipwrecked for three winter months in 60 CE, was a city that the Arab rulers later named Medina. Medina was the name taken from the northern Arabian city that had first accepted Mohammed as a prophet. Mecca had tried to murder Mohammad several times, whereas smaller, humble Medina had immediately accepted him and made him their leader. Medina was the precise location where Paul stayed with the Roman governor. It is right in the center of Malta. Paul was placed squarely in the center of the island he evangelized.

North African Arabs, centuries after Paul's three-month stay, later conquered and ruled from Malta's Medina for three hundred years before they were driven out by the Norman army and its knights in 1091 CE. Over nine hundred years earlier, the friendly, humble Maltese had accepted Paul of Tarsus. Now, conquering Norman Christians were received with joyous enthusiasm.

Malta's faith in Jesus of Nazareth had been repressed for so long. The Maltese were cheering, and their joy was so unrestrained that, moved by their emotions, Count Roger tore off the edge of his flag that was red and white and gave it to them.

That is why today the flag of Malta is red and white, in part because of the joy of the Maltese Christians, who could again openly practice their faith in the Jesus of Nazareth that Paul of Tarsus had originally brought them.

CHAPTER 37

The First Basic Training Sergeant of the Christian Church

Basic training has a special meaning for me after serving as basic training battalion chaplain at Fort Benning, Georgia, and basic training battalion chaplain at Fort Leonard Wood, Missouri, and being in the US Army for thirty years. My years of experience with officers and soldiers helped me develop an understanding of Paul of Tarsus that may be helpful to you in interpreting him.

Almost every soldier remembers the name of their basic training sergeant. Every Christian who reads the Christian scriptures remembers Paul of Tarsus for similar reasons. Paul's epistles are letters written to specific leaders (with the exception of the letter to the Ephesians) in specific churches. Paul was essentially the first basic training builder of church congregations, church members, church leaders, and church structure.

A church builder like Paul and a US Army basic training sergeant become every recruit's father and mother, big brother, Dutch uncle, friend, enemy, hero, villain, boss, bully, doctor, lawyer, and teacher.

Read Paul's letters closely. Paul is every single one of these persons and more to those early Christians. He loved every person and every congregation so much, and he was candid almost to the point of being rude. He loved them so much almost to the point of being embarrassing.

When we compare Paul to Peter, James, John, or someone else, we make a terrible mistake. Every apostle, prophet, evangelist, pastor, teacher, and church member has a slightly different ministry and function in the church. God does not make carbon copies. Everyone is unique. Every variation, every personality, and every church has a distinct place in honoring Jesus of Nazareth. Paul stands on his own merits as a Great Lion of God, but it is *all about Jesus*.

CHAPTER 38

Paul of Tarsus and the Ethics of the Stoic Philosophers

The founder and first teacher of the Stoic school of philosophy was Zeno of Citium (Cyprus) over three hundred years before the birth of Jesus of Nazareth. Both Tarsus and the Island of Cyprus were eastern Mediterranean trade centers and are relatively close to each other.

They had a history of trade relationships with each other for centuries before the Greek and Roman Empires. Some of their first trade was with the Phoenicians from Phoenicia, which is now called Lebanon.

Zeno himself was dark-skinned and fluent in the Greek language but made fun of by the Greeks for being a Phoenician. Zeno based his ethics on the Cynics who emphasized living a life of virtue. Zeno believed ethical behavior was in sync with nature and taught the importance of living a life of self-control and overcoming negative emotions, thereby finding peace in the world.

All of Zeno's ethical teachings agree with the foundational thinking of Ralph Waldo Emerson, the greatest philosopher that the United States of America has ever produced. All of Zeno's basic ethical thoughts also agree with the Hebrew scriptures, with the four gospels, and with the epistles of Peter, John, and Paul of Tarsus.

It is not surprising that Paul of Tarsus was significantly influenced by the Stoic philosophers because Antipater of Tarsus was born in Tarsus and died 130 years before the birth of Jesus of Nazareth. Antipater was a well-known Stoic philosopher who began teaching in Paul's own Roman city.

Stoic philosophers mirrored ancient Hebrew and Christian concepts of right living and moral behavior. Paul of Tarsus could not have helped learning about Antipater and being influenced by his teachings while growing up in Tarsus. Zeno and Antipater's works agreed with Paul's basic, ethical teachings. Paul was fluent in the koine Greek language prevalent in Tarsus and in Stoic philosophy and literature.

Even though Antipater of Tarsus lived in a world with dozens of gods and goddesses, Antipater taught there was one true God who was kind, sinless, and wished to help men and women. Like Socrates, he believed the Greek and Roman gods and goddesses were harmful to youth and the adult members of the ancient world because of their unethical behaviors.

Antipater's writings talk about the omniscience of God and the caring nature of God. He emphasized acting in a moral manner, rather than just talking about moral teachings. Living an honest life was one of Antipater's highest values.

Being in touch with nature was another subject on which all Stoic philosophers agreed with Hebrew and Christian thought. If you read each of the epistles attributed to Paul of Tarsus and then you read the Stoic philosophers, you will find that their values are present in each other's value systems.

After thoroughly reading the entire Bible using cross-references as a young Christian, I then began an individual, three-semester-hour, faculty-directed intensive study of several Stoic philosophers as a history major at Westmont College in Santa Barbara. It astonished me how the Stoics mirrored Paul's writings with the exception that they did not attribute anything to Jesus of Nazareth since they knew nothing about him.

Over three hundred years before Jesus's birth, the Stoics began writing about ethics with a clarity and preciseness that prepared the ancient world for Jesus's teachings and Paul's writings. As a Christian, I do not think that the timing was by chance. Stoics prepared the way for the Christian message and for the epistles of Paul of Tarsus.

Grace Interdenominational Church where I grew up in Santa Barbara, California, had Baptists, Pentecostals, Catholics,

Mennonites, Presbyterians, Brethren, Disciples of Christ, Presbyterians, and several other groups, and yet their Christian faith all agreed.

The basic Stoic ethical teachings of Antipater of Tarsus most assuredly agreed with Paul's understandings of Hebrew ethics in his youth and his later ethics in his Christian epistles. Zeno, Antipater, and the Stoic teachings were a significant part of Paul's letters and agreed with Jesus of Nazareth's ethical teachings. They were part and parcel of the Hebrew ethical values out of which Jesus operated.

There was one Stoic philosopher I appreciated the most. His name was Epictetus. Years later, I was pleased to learn that Emperor Marcus Aurelius and those around him also thought Epictetus was one of the best of the Stoic teachers. Here are some of Epictetus's teachings:

> No one is free who is not master of themselves ... Circumstances don't make the man, they only reveal him to himself ... You are not your body and hair-style. You are what you choose. If your choices are beautiful, you will be beautiful ... We do not know the stories behind the actions of others, so we need to be patient with others and suspend judgement of them, recognizing the limits of our understanding ... Deliberate much before saying or doing anything, for you will not have the power of recalling what is said or done.

If you study the writings of Paul of Tarsus closely, you will see again that Epictetus's words parallel many of Paul's teachings. If you study the life and words of Jesus of Nazareth, you will see that they also parallel Jesus's thoughts.

If you study the lyrical passages of the Hebrew scriptures, particularly Psalms, Proverbs, and Isaiah, you will note that Epictetus's words echo their thoughts. The Stoics are one of the reasons Paul's words and Jesus's words are timeless and have such great power. Truth is truth no matter what century.

Summing it up, I believe that in God's infinite plan, Zeno and the Greek-speaking Stoic school of thought not only spread the wisdom of the Cynics and the wisdom of the Stoics but also helped to prepare for the spread of the wisdom of the teachings of Jesus of Nazareth and the incredibly well-read and brilliant writings of Paul of Tarsus, his most widely traveled, articulate apostle.

CHAPTER 39

The Time Was Right for Paul's Message

The Roman Empire was at its zenith when Jesus of Nazareth was born and when Paul of Tarsus was born just a few years later. Roman armies had subdued bandits and robbers on the amazing road system that they built and maintained. There was active shipping throughout the empire from Arabia to Africa, India, and Asia. Commerce was flourishing.

At the same time, the Senate in Rome was steadily being weakened by repeated dictatorships and was on the cusp of deterioration when the new heresy of Judaism, called Christianity, appeared. The Roman Army had started to become diluted of some of its patriotism and energy by more and more non-Roman, non-Greek soldiers. Slaves were making the lives of the wealthy more indulgent, less disciplined, and increasingly selfish.

Socrates's truth that the Greek and Roman gods and goddesses were immoral and unethical was gradually becoming accepted since his death by hemlock in 399 BCE. His willingness to accept death and to die for the truth was an inspirational precursor to Jesus of Nazareth and his willingness to die for truth on the cross more than four hundred years later.

Mystery religions were becoming popular, thus weakening ties to past gods and goddesses. Some of the mystery religions involved blood sacrifices of animals as part of their membership rites, preparing the way for Holy Communion, which emphasized the shed blood of Jesus of Nazareth on the cross.

Paul's Greek and Roman studies in Tarsus and his Hebrew and Jewish studies in Jerusalem had prepared him to be a man for all seasons. Greek and Roman cultures existed and were helpful in spreading the Good News of how Jesus of Nazareth was indeed the long-awaited Messiah.

In his epistles, Paul clearly understood the cultures of his day. Paul's communication skills stirred the hearts of kings, generals, and ordinary people to think seriously about Jesus's appearance at that moment in world history. Paul's death in Rome was his final and most powerful message. Paul's valiant death sealed the truth of his message forever.

Nero, the Roman emperor at the time of Paul's crucifixion in Rome, has gone down in history as being beyond evil. He murdered his mother, his wife, and his stepbrother, and then Nero executed Paul and Peter. He persecuted the followers of Jesus whenever he was able. There is an ancient Christian proverb: "The blood of the martyrs is the seed of the church." Jesus's blood, Paul's blood, and Peter's blood were the rich soil out of which the church grew. *It is all about Jesus*.

CHAPTER 40

Peter Had Read the Epistles
of Paul of Tarsus

In 2 Peter 3:14–18 (MSG), Peter said,

> Our good brother Paul, who was given much
> wisdom in these matters, (about the "Master's
> patient restraint for what it is: salvation" 3:15)
> he refers to this in all his letters, and has written
> you essentially the same thing.

Peter continues saying some things Paul writes are difficult to
understand. Irresponsible people who don't know what they
are talking about twist them every which way. They do it to the
rest of the scriptures too, destroying themselves as they do it.

There are several important things that have too often been
missed and overlooked in Peter's statement about Paul of
Tarsus. The first is that Peter and Paul essentially agree that
all followers of Jesus must "Do your very best to be found living
at your best, in purity and peace."

The second important thing is that Peter and Paul agreed on the issue of "salvation." Peter, the early church, and Paul believe that a person must be "born from above," as Jesus stated, and have a personal salvation experience just as both Peter and Paul had their values and their lives totally turned around toward goodness, light, forgiveness, and God's love.

The third is that Paul is at times "difficult to understand." For example, Paul's legal arguments in the book of Romans are very esoteric and precise and full of such deep logic as he tries to explain a person's inner struggles about what it means to live a normal life while trying wholeheartedly to follow God.

The fourth important thing Peter mentions is that even in Peter's age, "Irresponsible people ... twist ... every which way" Paul's written words and "destroy themselves" and those who hear those twisted words. Christian history is full of examples of such irresponsibility that has dreadfully harmed so many lives.

One trenchant example of twisting Paul's words and Jesus's words was how the present Christian churches and the early church councils have had to repeatedly guard against the subtle but potentially devastating heresy, which has always existed since the early church, that Jesus was not God in the flesh.

Too often, Jesus was seen in the ancient world and is seen in our modern world only as a young man who was a great prophet and misguidedly thought he was the Messiah. Jesus was also misrepresented as appearing to be human but really not being a flesh-and-blood person. These teachings take away Jesus's flesh-and-blood sacrifice on the cross and make Jesus ethereal and not a real human being.

The fifth important thing Peter says is that he and the early church regarded Paul's writings as *scriptures*. What this means is that long before 325 years after the birth of Jesus, when the canon of Christian scriptures was solidified at the Council of Nicaea, far before that time, while Peter was still alive, Paul's letters were considered Christian scripture.

For early Christians, the Torah, the Biblical accounts about God, the historical accounts of the Hebrew peoples, Psalms, Proverbs, and the writings of all the Hebrew prophets were regarded as scripture. Later, the Gospels of Matthew, Mark, Luke, and John became the center of the Christian Bible with Christians saying that the Hebrew scriptures pointed to Jesus, the gospels about Jesus were at the center of the Bible, and the epistles pointed back to Jesus. As mentioned earlier, Paul probably wrote the first book or epistle in the Christian scriptures. The gospels and the rest of the New Testament came later.

Peter concludes this passage with the same concepts as Paul of Tarsus, "Grow in Grace and understanding of our Master and Savior, Jesus Christ." Peter echoes the words of Paul of Tarsus, who repeatedly said that the Christian message was not about Peter or Paul or Apollos any other human being. *The message is all about Jesus of Nazareth.*

CHAPTER 41

Why Paul's Letters May
Seem Anti-Semitic

Understanding the first-century Jewish attitudes toward Paul of Tarsus is foundational to understanding Paul's letters. Few Christians are fully aware of the many reasons why Jewish leaders of synagogues during Paul's missionary journeys had many understandable conflicts not only with Paul's teachings but also with his behaviors.

If a man like Paul came into our synagogue or church or mosque or temple and began proselytizing our members to another faith, any member of our congregation would be antagonistic toward him. Paul was very direct and forceful. Luke, in the book of Acts, and Paul, in his epistles, often mention persecution from Jews in these synagogues who did not believe Jesus was the Messiah. Their reactions were understandable, but this gives Christians no right to be anti-Semitic.

Remember the historical fact that there were also many Jews before Jesus who claimed to be the Messiah and were found out to be imposters. If the Romans didn't get them, the Jews would try to stone them. It would be hard for Paul not to mention negative things about Jews who had stoned and opposed him. It was hard for Paul to dismiss those who had verbally abused him and those who had physically attacked him from city to city on his missionary journeys.

Paul was not anti-Semitic. He was a Jew himself. His comments too often have been interpreted by Christians in an anti-Semitic way that Paul had not intended. The entire Christian community in Jerusalem, with a few exceptions, was Jewish.

Jews did not murder Jesus. Misreading Paul would lead a casual reader to surmise this. Religious leaders murdered Jesus by pressuring the Romans to do their dirty work. The average Jewish person loved Jesus. Israel is a small country. Word of Jesus's teachings, healings, and casting out of demons spread like wildfire. People came from far and wide to see and hear him.

After the wedding in Cana of Galilee, the servants who had seen him turn the water into the best wine could barely wait to tell everyone about his first miracle. The feeding of five thousand men, as well as an unknown number of women and children, really mobilized people to hear him and love him. Jesus's words and actions could not be repressed. News about Jesus was on everyone's lips.

Jesus's disciples told him that the Jewish people were saying that he was either Elijah or one of the prophets. Even King Herod thought he was John the Baptist come back to life. Ordinary Jews thought he might be the Messiah who would drive the Romans out of Judea and set up a new kingdom. Ordinary men and women had no desire to kill Jesus or to harm his followers.

Jews were not "Christ-killers." The Sadducees, who controlled the temple and the sacrifices, were the ones who wanted to get rid of Jesus, not the Jewish people as a whole. This is a huge misunderstanding of Paul's writings. This misunderstanding has led to incredible persecution of Jews by so-called Christians, by followers of Islam, by Hitler, and by many others to this very day.

CHAPTER 42

Martin Luther's Anti-Semitism as It Relates to Paul

Martin Luther steeped himself in Paul's epistles and brought about the Protestant Reformation. Luther tried to honor Jesus of Nazareth as seen through Paul's teachings of salvation by faith and by the grace of God and not through human works. He therefore could not have missed Paul's negative comments about Jewish leaders repeatedly opposing him and physically harming him. Luther's comments about Jewish people are classic examples of misreading Paul of Tarsus. Luther ended up having a livid hatred of Jews.

Early in his life, Luther had tried to convert Jewish people and failed. Early on, he had expressed concern about the history of Jews being persecuted, but when he was unsuccessful in converting them, he began to speak against the Jewish faith and its followers. He criticized them and then lowered his standards to propose the active persecution of Jews.

Paul would totally disagree with what Luther suggested in his pamphlet *On the Jews and Their Lies*. In the twenty-first century, it is almost unbelievable what Luther suggested: set fire to their synagogues and their schools, destroy their houses, take their books and the Talmud from them, not allow their rabbis to teach, not allow Jews to own businesses, keep Jews out of the banking industry, make Jews do physical work, and make Jews leave the country as other European nations had done.

Luther's suggestions in this book go far beyond anything Paul of Tarsus would suggest or even think of doing. No wonder Hitler and the German people went wild tormenting and killing Jews. Their own prophet, Martin Luther, recommended this persecution plainly.

Centuries before Luther, Mohammed had a similar experience. He had moved to Medina to escape death and persecution in Mecca. Medina at that time had two Arab tribes and three Jewish tribes. Mohammed spent a lot of time discussing spirituality with these tribes. Like Luther, he tried to convert them to his faith in Allah. The Jews held steadfast to their faith in Yahweh and Elohim.

When one tribe revolted against his leadership, he punished the tribe as traitors and expelled the other two tribes. Mohammed did not rail about the tribes in the specific, cruel, torturous manor that Luther did. Some of Luther's rancor came from Paul's repeated defamation of Jews in the epistles. Mohammed's rancor was solely related to being betrayed in a battle and war against Mecca.

CHAPTER 43

Martin Luther, Grace, Faith, Paul, and It Is All about Jesus

Martin Luther loved the Roman Catholic Church. He joined a monastery and then became a professor in a theological seminary. He lectured on Paul's writings in Romans and Galatians and began to understand Paul's emphasis on the salvation of God not by works but by the sheer grace of God.

Luther gradually began to realize how the church legal system emphasized human actions and not the redeeming forgiveness of Jesus on the cross. When Johann Tetzel, a Dominican friar, began to sell indulgences for the forgiveness of sins for the building of St. Peter's in Rome, Luther had to stand up for Jesus of Nazareth, as understood by Paul of Tarsus. It was the grace of God by faith in Jesus's sacrifice on the cross. Money could not purchase forgiveness. It was all about Jesus.

Luther wrote his ninety-five theses based on Paul's concept of "salvation though faith alone" (*Sola Fide*). Luther then took it one step further. In place of the power of the pope and the church councils, Luther said the scriptures, not church tradition, were the final source of authority (*Sola Scriptura*).

Luther's struggle took place during a period of budding German nationalism versus Italian nationalism as seen in Rome and the pope. The printing press had also been invented, and Luther's words could be read in German by ordinary men and women. John Huss, one hundred years before Luther, had taught very similar things but had no printing press to help him.

Luther then went to the extreme with following Paul's faith and grace concepts. Luther called the book of James, "an epistle of straw" because it talked about works proving a person had a faith in God. "You say you have faith? Show me your faith by your works" (James 2:18).

Luther overemphasized Paul of Tarsus's writings, just as he had misread Paul regarding the Jews, as discussed in the previous chapter. Many Christians today also overemphasize Paul's writings.

It was beginning with Luther's lifetime that Paul of Tarsus and his words in his epistles began to be followed and often emphasized more than the words of Jesus of Nazareth. The Luther/Paul faith versus the Epistle of James works standoff still continues to this day.

I have no doubt Paul, if he were alive today, would say something like this: "I was sent to bring the message of God's love through Jesus to Jews and non-Jews. Before that, I was arresting Jews who followed Jesus. Today I honor and serve Jesus of Nazareth, and I am willing to die for him."

Luther opened the door for so many to set their eyes on Jesus and not on works. Paul revolutionized the ancient world, and Luther revolutionized the modern world by emphasizing Jesus. It is imperative that Christians thank God for Paul of Tarsus and thank God for Martin Luther but honor first Jesus of Nazareth. *It is all about Jesus.*

CHAPTER 44

Paul's Comments and Teachings Regarding Women

Paul was a creature of his age. Women were treated as second-class citizens. It was not uncommon in ancient Rome and Greece when one entertained an overnight guest to give his wife to his guest for the evening.

This was the hedonistic world that Paul lived in. This custom goes very much against the Hebrew teachings on marriage, which Paul followed. It also shows the lack of respect the ancient world had for women. Paul was adamantly opposed to this. He greatly honored the sanctity of marriage.

When I visited a very large Orthodox synagogue in the Midwest as a seminary student, I found that the women were seated on one side, and the men were seated on the other. The same is true in Islamic mosques. Even today, there is a separation and implied denigration of women not only in strict Jewish circles but in Roman Catholic and Eastern Orthodox Christianity and in many Protestant and independent Christian churches.

Reformed Jewish congregations today treat women as equal human beings.

When we look at all the books in the Christian scriptures that Paul was reported to have written, we see a significant disconnect between how Paul wrote or was purported to have written about women and how Jesus of Nazareth talked to and treated women. This one subject alone has generated volumes of comments and countercomments. Compare Jesus's treatment of women to Paul's words about women for yourself.

Jesus spoke with the woman at the well in Samaria. He asked her to get him some water. The woman was astonished on several accounts: First, it was amazing to her that Jesus had spoken to her because she was a woman. Second, she was even more astonished that he had spoken to her because she was a Samaritan. Jews avoided Samaritans.

Third, she was amazed that he was in her Samaritan town. Jews never went near Samaritan towns and villages because although they had some elements of Judaism, they did not believe in the whole of the Hebrew culture or the entire Hebrew scriptures. Fourth, Jesus respected her even though he knew of her promiscuous past with four husbands and living with a Samaritan man who was not her husband.

Fifth, and perhaps her greatest surprise, was that he accurately, divinely knew her specific past personal history. How could he have known she had been married several times and was living with a man who was not her husband? She then realized that he was indeed a living prophet of great insight and spiritual power and might even be the Messiah.

She went and told everyone in her Samaritan village. This caused Jesus to stay there two more days, preparing them for the later Good News of his sacrifice on the cross and his salvation. There still exists a small enclave of eight hundred Samaritans in Israel to this day. The disciples were amazed not only that he had talked with a Samaritan woman, but he stayed and taught Samaritans in their own, ritually impure to Jews village.

Issues about Paul's thoughts toward women surface in many different areas. Some Bible scholars see certain books attributed to Paul as possibly being written by someone else, but technical scholarship aside, the average Christian believer generally sees every book attributed to Paul as being straight from Paul and so have most Christians for almost two thousand years.

Paul therefore is quoted as saying,

> ***Therefore I want the men in every place to pray, lifting up holy hands without anger and dispute. Likewise also the women should adorn themselves in appropriate clothing, with modesty and self-control, not with braided***

hair and gold jewelry or pearls or expensive clothing, but with good deeds which are fitting for women who profess godliness. A woman must learn in quietness with all submission. But I do not permit a woman to teach or to exercise authority over a man, but to remain quiet. For Adam was formed first, then Eve, and Adam was not deceived, but the woman, because she was deceived, came into transgression. But she will be saved through the bearing of children, if she continues in faith and love and holiness with self-control. (I Timothy 2:8–15 LEB)

These words are interpreted by many women and men as making women into second-class citizens. As mentioned earlier, several books could be written just on this one Paul/women theme.

My concern is that we consider Jesus's interactions with his mother and all the other women in his life and that we better understand Jesus's teachings in general on marriage and women and children.

When in doubt, it is wise to take Jesus's approach and not focus on everything Paul said about women to Timothy or to the churches in Ephesus or in Corinth and so on. Paul was a faithful servant, a learned Pharisee, and a student of Gamaliel, but to Christians, Jesus is the Messiah, the Son of the Living God in the flesh.

Looking precisely at what Jesus said and did with women is a good counterpoint to the words of Paul and Paul's close followers today. In addition to the Samaritan woman story, the Gospel of Mark, chapter five, tells the intimate, loving story of how Jesus treated the hemorrhaging woman. Jesus's kindness and gentleness is so instructive.

The woman was desperate. She had been bleeding for twelve years. Menstruating women were unclean according to Jewish law. In the huge crowd, she also went totally against Middle Eastern and Jewish law when she touched a man who was not her husband. She believed touching Jesus's robe would heal her. When Jesus asked who had touched him and she fell at his feet, Jesus told her that her faith had healed her, and he blessed her and told her to go in peace.

In another instance, in Luke 21, Jesus saw a widow who had given her last two pennies to the temple treasury. Jesus said it was the only money she had. Jesus then used her as an example to the men with him of how they needed to give their all to God.

In John 8, a woman had committed adultery. Jesus first pointed out to the men who accused her that they were not without similar inward and outward faults. All the men who were going to stone her left. (Notice they did not even think of stoning the man who had also committed adultery.) Jesus restores her dignity and tells her to go on her way free and alive and not to sin again.

Many men have taken Paul's letters and supposed comments on women, quoted them, taught about them, and used them as a tool to denigrate women. They have used passages like I Corinthians 14:34–35 (NOA) to make women subordinate.

> Women should be silent in the churches. For they are not permitted to speak, but should be subordinate, as the law also says. If there is anything they desire to know, let them ask their husbands at home. For it is shameful for a woman to speak in church.

Thus, Paul unwittingly influenced the Christian church specifically and society in general, giving his permission to continue to treat women as second-class citizen class citizens. This was just the opposite of Jesus of Nazareth. He treated women with respect.

CHAPTER 45

Paul of Tarsus and His Obsession with Sin

Jesus of Nazareth was not obsessed with sin. Jesus did not minimize the Ten Commandments or the Jewish social laws of his day. Rather he said that he had come to fulfill the law but that "not one jot or one tittle of the law" would he change. Jesus's emphasis was on the love, mercy, and forgiveness of God. In other words, he was much more balanced on the issue of sin than Paul of Tarsus.

Romans 1:24–32 gives a detailed account of some of Paul's many sin obsessions:

> So God said, in effect, "If that's what you want, that's what you get." It wasn't long before they were living in a pigpen, smeared with filth, filthy inside and out. And all this because they traded the true God for a fake god, and worshiped the god they made instead of the God who made them—the God we bless, the God who blesses us. Oh, yes! Worse followed. Refusing to know

God, they soon didn't know how to be human either—women didn't know how to be women, men didn't know how to be men. Sexually confused, they abused and defiled one another, women with women, men with men—all lust, no love. And then they paid for it, oh, how they paid for it—emptied of God and love, godless and loveless wretches. Since they didn't bother to acknowledge God, God quit bothering them and let them run loose. And then all hell broke loose: rampant evil, grabbing and grasping, vicious backstabbing. They made life hell on earth with their envy, wanton killing, bickering, and cheating. Look at them: mean-spirited, venomous, fork-tongued God-bashers. Bullies, swaggerers, insufferable windbags! They keep inventing new ways of wrecking lives. They ditch their parents when they get in the way. Stupid, slimy, cruel, cold-blooded. And it's not as if they don't know better. They know perfectly well they're spitting in God's face.

Paul seems to be particularly obsessed with sexual sins. He had lists of people in his epistles who were sinners and would not make it into heaven. Jesus was not as obsessed with sin. The Greek word for sin was "short of God's glory."

Paul appeared to be taking the ancient Hebrew stance that adulterers and gays and lesbians needed to be stoned to death. This is not necessarily the case, but it is important in understanding Paul to know that even though the Romans officially made marriage an important thing that the eastern, Greek-speaking half of the Roman Empire and Rome itself were sexual cesspools.

In the city of Tarsus and in Jerusalem's history, there was a plethora of fertility temples to Ashtoreth and Venus complete with male and female temple sexual partners who were an official part of these fertility rites. The last Hebrew prophets in the Hebrew scriptures say that this was one of the reasons Jerusalem and all of Israel were destroyed before the Babylonian captivity.

The word "Lesbian" comes from the Greek island of Lesbos. Both Phillip of Macedonia and his son, Alexander the Great, had male lovers. Alexander became king of Macedonia early at age twenty because Phillip was murdered by his jilted homosexual lover.

But it gets worse. Little children were often used as sexual toys. This still occurs in Afghanistan openly, but it happens in virtually every country in today's world, inhumane child sex trafficking. Paul's world was no different. It was full of sexual improprieties.

In the next chapter in this book, we will see how Paul himself appeared obsessed with being celibate and openly wrote how he wished other church leaders were not married and were also celibate. Paul said one of the most terrible things about marriage ever written in Hebrew scripture or Christian scripture: "It is better to marry than to burn with lust."

In Paul's defense, he also had lists of positive things, such as in Philippians 4:8–9:

> Summing it all up, friends, I'd say you'll do best by filling your minds and meditating on things true, noble, reputable, authentic, compelling, gracious—the best, not the worst; the beautiful, not the ugly; things to praise, not things to curse. Put into practice what you learned from me, what you heard and saw and realized. Do that, and God, who makes everything work together, will work you into his most excellent harmonies.

Paul was a very complicated, complex person with aspects of Jewish, Greek, and Roman customs, thoughts, and cultures and languages constantly coursing through his writings, thoughts, and epistles. It should be noted that Paul's description of love in I Corinthians 13 is one of the most lyrical and foundational ever written. It ends with these wonderful words, "Faith, Hope, and Love, and the greatest of these is Love."

CHAPTER 46

Jesus's Teaching on Celibacy versus Paul's Comments on Celibacy

Marriage is mentioned seventeen times in the four gospels. In John 2, Jesus performed his first miracle when his family and his disciples were invited to a marriage at Cana of Galilee. To keep the bride and bridegroom from being embarrassed and to please his mother, Jesus turned many gallons of water into the best wine. Marriage was important then and now. It is the pillar of most societies on earth.

Here are Paul's comments in I Corinthians 9 (MSG). Note in verses 7–11, Paul takes a stand for not being married. Also notice his words about divorce. He says that his teachings on divorce are not his words but rather "the Master's Command." Even in his discussion about marriage, Paul defers to Jesus of Nazareth:

> It's good for a man to have a wife, and for a woman to have a husband. Sexual drives are strong, but marriage is strong enough to contain

them and provide for a balanced and fulfilling sexual life in a world of sexual disorder. The marriage bed must be a place of mutuality—the husband seeking to satisfy his wife, the wife seeking to satisfy her husband. Marriage is not a place to "stand up for your rights." Marriage is a decision to serve the other, whether in bed or out.

Abstaining from sex is permissible for a period of time if you both agree to it, and if it's for the purposes of prayer and fasting—but only for such times. Then come back together again. Satan has an ingenious way of tempting us when we least expect it. I'm not, understand, commanding these periods of abstinence—only providing my best counsel if you should choose them.

Sometimes I wish everyone were single like me—a simpler life in many ways! But celibacy is not for everyone any more than marriage is. God gives the gift of the single life to some, the gift of the married life to others. I do, though, tell the unmarried and widows that singleness might well be the best thing for them, as it has been for me.

But if they can't manage their desires and emotions, they should by all means go ahead and get married. The difficulties of marriage are preferable by far to a sexually tortured life as a single. And if you are married, stay married. *This is the Master's command, not mine.* If a wife should leave her husband, she must either remain single or else come back and make things right with him. And a husband has no right to get rid of his wife.

In this passage of scripture, Paul is rather balanced about celibacy. It is to be noted in the passage that Paul was very direct about sexual matters within marriage. This was rather important because in the ancient world of the Roman Empire, marital sex was one of several often deviant sexual behaviors.

CHAPTER 47

The Thankful Heart of Paul of Tarsus

In his epistles or letters in the Christian scriptures, Paul constantly gives thanks: "God be thanked" (Romans 6:17); "I thank God" (Romans 7:25); "Thanks be unto God" (II Corinthians 9:15); "We give thanks to God" (Colossians 1:3); "Giving thanks unto the Father" (Colossians 1:12); and "We thank God without ceasing" (I Thessalonians 2:13). Paul and Silas praised God in prison in chains.

Hindrek Taavet Taimla of Voru, Estonia, writes in the *Upper Room* (February 25, 2015, page 68),

> Psychologists emphasize that a disposition of gratitude promotes healthy living and joy. The Bible—especially the Book of Psalms—is full of gratitude and praise for all of God's good works. Paul expresses thankfulness in all of his letters. How true it is that even a glimpse of the suffering, death and resurrection of Christ accomplished for us can fill us with joy unspeakable.

Hindrek has very good spiritual and psychological insight when he points out that Paul had an attitude of gratitude about virtually every good thing and every difficult thing that happened to him in his work as an apostle (or "sent one").

Jesus taught that it was *overflow* of love and thankfulness not obsessive *overwork* that would sustain the life and long-term effectiveness of his followers. "Out of your innermost being shall flow rivers of living water" (John 7:38 KJV).

Thankfulness is clearly one of the things that kept Paul inspired, active, and positive during all of his difficult missionary work of being stoned, beaten, arrested, and demeaned as he worked among Jews and Gentiles, sharing the life of Jesus right up until his very last breath.

Enthusiasm was not lacking in Paul. At first, it was enthusiasm to rigorously enforce and fulfill all the laws of Orthodox Judaism by imposing his will on the heretical Jews called Christians. After years of fellowship with the remaining apostles and believers in Jerusalem (Paul's years of training are often not mentioned when teaching about Paul of Tarsus), Paul's growing faith mellowed and he began to understand it was God's grace and faith, as seen in Romans and Galatians, and not the Jewish laws that were important since no one could fulfill all that the law required without God's mercy and forgiveness.

This leads us to ponder, after a few more chapters, the teachings of Gamaliel in a following chapter. Gamaliel was Paul's wise teacher. He taught Paul for many years as a young Jewish student in Jerusalem to be thankful for the Torah, Abraham, Moses, the Prophets, and all of the Hebrew scriptures.

CHAPTER 48

Isaiah, Paul, and the Gifts of the Holy Spirit

Many Christians are not aware of the list Isaiah makes of the gifts of the Spirit of God in Isaiah 11:1–4 (MSG): "Life-giving wisdom, direction, strength, knowledge, fear of God, joy, and delight." Isaiah was speaking of the use of these gifts within the temple, the synagogues, and the Jewish community as a whole.

In contrast, Paul of Tarsus was describing the gifts he was seeing in the early church after the Day of Pentecost. After he described these gifts, he taught the early Christians how these gifts were to operate in their interactions with each other and in their worship services. Isaiah's list was valid but more general. Paul's list was much more specific and practical.

In I Corinthians 12 (MSG), he lists the gifts: "Wise counsel, clear understanding, simple trust, healing the sick, miraculous acts, proclamation, distinguishing between the spirits, tongues (in part praise languages), and interpretation of tongues."

If it was not was not for Paul of Tarsus, the first-century Christian community would not have such a detailed list. Christians would have only a general idea of the gifts, similar to those listed in Isaiah. Paul saw and experienced many of these gifts of the Holy Spirit in operation within his own life and within the life of the early churches.

This again reminds us of the truth that one person (Paul) with an experience is worth one hundred people with a theory. There is nothing theoretical about Paul's detailed descriptions of these gifts in his writings to the individual churches. It is practical advice.

Paul was not in the Upper Room when the Holy Spirit "fell with tongues of fire" on over three hundred early Christians. They began praising God in languages which they did not know, and their praises were verified by believers all over the known world who were there and spoke those languages as seen in Acts 2 (MSG): Parthians, Medes, Elamites, Mesopotamians, Judeans, Cappadocians, people from Pontus and Asia, Cretans, Phrygians, Pamphylians, Egyptians, Libyans, Cyrenaicans, Romans, and Arabians. That is a huge number of eyewitnesses.

CHAPTER 49

These Gifts of the Holy Spirit
Are Still Taking Place

All of these gifts of the Holy Spirit are still happening today throughout the world. From time to time, like in the Upper Room, God is still being spontaneously praised by people who have no knowledge of what language they are speaking. People are still being healed. Wise counsel and miraculous acts are quietly being done in Christian communities and in individual believers' lives.

Like Paul and many Christians, I have been blessed to see with my own eyes and hear with my own ears many of these gifts. I hope in reading this book you are inspired to seek any number of these gifts to lead people to a faith in a loving Lord. The only proviso is that when that gift that you want comes to you, then you have a responsibility to use it to glorify Jesus of Nazareth just as Paul of Tarsus tried to do in every way he could.

List any one of these gifts of the Holy Spirit and then read about Paul's life closely in his epistles. Almost every one of those gifts was active in Paul's life at one time or another. You, as a follower of Jesus Christ, have the potential for every one of these to be active in your life also.

Christians owe a deep debt to Paul because Peter, John, James, Apollos, Barnabus, Mark, or Phillip did not write about these specific gifts as did Paul of Tarsus. These early leaders had seen these gifts in action. They had probably had them operate in their own lives from time to time, but they did not write about them. Paul of Tarsus deserves our profound thanks for waking us up to the numinous, awesome things God did and is still doing among the followers of Jesus of Nazareth, just as Jesus himself did.

CHAPTER 50

Paul of Tarsus and His Wise Teacher Named Gamaliel

It is so important in one's spiritual life and in every single aspect of everyday life to be balanced. As I am working the rough draft of this book into a more finished product, one of my former students stopped me at my health club. "Dr. Cobb, do you remember me from ten years ago?"

I told him that his face was familiar but asked him to help me with his name. He told me and then said, "I took your class on ethics, and that class changed my life. I have been clean and sober for ten years now."

I asked what aspect of my class helped him the most. "You taught me to be balanced and said that even when I held a strong opinion to always listen to the other side. I have been doing that. I used to be so extreme on one side or the other. I got married. I have a good job. Thank you for helping me find balance."

Gamaliel was so balanced in his approach to Judaism, to Jesus of Nazareth, and to the new Christian movement. Gamaliel urged the Jewish council called the Sanhedrin not to overreact to Jesus's teachings and life, and later, he urged them not to overreact to this new Christian faith that was growing in Jerusalem.

The Sanhedrin listened to him because he was a well-respected teacher of Judaism in Jerusalem but did not follow his advice. The Sanhedrin had Jesus murdered by the Romans. They also had begun to arrest and murder the Jewish Christian leaders of the Jerusalem church, starting with Stephen and James.

When he first enters the picture in the book of Acts, Paul was obviously not following Gamaliel's example of moderation. He was not listening to both sides. He was going out of his way to arrest Christians, but like the leaders in the Sanhedrin, Paul of Tarsus still greatly respected his beloved teacher, Gamaliel.

Ancient Judaism centered primarily on rituals, laws, and living a Godly and ethical life in this present world. Sadducees did not believe in life after death even though Job, the book of Psalms, and other Jewish scriptures repeatedly mention the possibility of life after death.

The Sadducees followed an ancient Jewish concept of "Sheol." Sheol was an underworld place where the souls of the dead went. Ancient Hebrew thought about life after death was that if a person lived a good life, he or she would be remembered long after he or she was gone. This memory was the person's eternal footprint.

They felt everlasting life meant one would be remembered by people still living, family and friends. If a person achieved the status of Moses, Elijah, or David, his or her eternal legacy would live forever. The Sadducees fought for this ancient belief.

A newer Jewish sect, the Pharisees, had begun to believe in the existence of the life to come. This was precisely what Jesus taught, that there was an entirely new existence in the life to come. Jesus called God his "father" and said there would be a "place" for everyone who followed him in heaven. This was even beyond the Pharisees' concept. It angered the Sadducees and was concerning to the Pharisees.

Luke reports that many Jews believed in Jesus after Lazarus was raised from the dead. Later, after so many hundreds of people had seen Jesus alive after his crucifixion, this belief in a life after death greatly increased in Jerusalem among the Jewish Christians.

It is interesting that Paul, expertly trained by Gamaliel in Jewish pharisaical beliefs of a life to come, would side with the Sadducees and not with the Pharisees to persecute early Jewish Christians. (The book of Acts records that many Pharisees later became believers in Jesus.)

Gamaliel had been following in the footsteps of another beloved teacher, Hillel, his great-grandfather, who had first begun his Hebrew training school in Jerusalem. Paul's rough, uncompromising Judaism might have been even more unbalanced without the moderating influence of Gamaliel. Gamaliel's teaching not to persecute Christians because one "might be fighting with God" was not in Paul's early thinking when he was named Saul.

Luke's book of Acts shows that Gamaliel saw the wisdom of the life and teachings of Jesus. Gamaliel urged caution. He believed that Jesus's teachings might be much more valid than many other Pharisees and Sadducees realized.

Gamaliel undoubtedly mourned the murder of Jesus on the cross because he had pointedly warned the Sanhedrin not to kill Jesus. Gamaliel realized that their murderous decision was influenced not by the teachings of the Hebrew scriptures but rather by temple politics and power and money.

After Jesus's death, Luke mentions how Gamaliel continued to warn the Sanhedrin and the Jewish leaders to leave alone those Jews who were trying to follow Jesus's teachings. He told the council that in persecuting them, they might be trying to stop something that was of God. What a prophetic statement that was.

Why Paul of Tarsus refused to follow Gamaliel's advice himself is a question that no one can accurately answer. Paul was young, full of himself, and full of what he thought was the righteous, vigorous, and only correct truth about Judaism.

This same tendency is seen in the twenty-first century by young Protestants attacking Roman Catholics, young Hindus attacking followers of the Sikh faith, Jews being attacked by many different groups, Buddhists attacking followers of Islam, young Islamic men attacking Christians, and Christians attacking others. Violence in the name of God is far too common in youthful followers of any faith, as vividly shown in Paul of Tarsus's early life. Gamaliel was clearly against such violence.

CHAPTER 51

Jesus as Understood by Jesus

It is so incredibly important that we understand Jesus as understood by Jesus in his own life and teachings and not as understood by Paul of Tarsus. Paul never personally met Jesus before his resurrection; nevertheless, Paul gives us good insights into Jesus's life, good insights into Jesus's teachings, and good insights into how to follow Jesus in our daily walk.

Yet in Christian living with personal standards and with historical accuracy and clarity of thought, it is very important to go back to the *original source*: Jesus of Nazareth. It is so very important to go back to the *original source documents*, which are Matthew, Mark, Luke, and John. Repeatedly, Paul, in his writings, totally agrees with the fact that Jesus is the center of everything. In Paul's core essence and in several of his epistles, he repeatedly says to look at Jesus and not at Paul.

Too often, the gospels and the life of Jesus are taught as understood by Paul and not as understood by Jesus. Western Christians tend to have a Greek and Roman, left-brain understanding of society and of the Good News of the life of Jesus. A more accurate, Hebrew, Aramaic, holistic, right-brain understanding of God's love is how Jesus operated.

Greek and Roman words are left-brain, logical, sequential, and practical. Aramaic and Hebrew are more sweeping, universal, and emotional and look deeply at eternal issues. Jesus's words and life were much more encompassing than the Greek language.

This means that the life and words of Jesus are more powerful, more emotionally gripping, and more visual than any Greek or Roman Latin language can ever possibly explain. Jesus, as understood by Jesus's own teachings, is the best and finest representation of God-in-the-flesh. Aramaic-English translations of the gospels can be helpful in understanding Jesus.

The Western world would not have been as quickly Christianized if it had not been for Paul of Tarsus. Paul explained Jesus in a way that Greeks and Romans could understand. He did this in their cities, and then their trade routes and their military conquests and explorations efficiently spread that message of God's love. To grow deeper into the Christian faith, it is important to go beyond Paul's easier understandings to the original profundities of Jesus's life and words as understood though his more profound life, teachings, and actions.

A good example of Jesus's simple profundity is when he took the little children in his arms and told the disciples not to forbid them coming to him, because children are examples of people who follow God with a childlike faith and childlike trust. Right now, visualize Jesus telling his disciples this with his arms around these little ones. Visualize the loving look on Jesus's face as he picked up each child to illustrate his point. His actions go far more loving and deeper. They are far beyond concrete Greek and Roman words.

I would encourage you, if you are a follower of Jesus of Nazareth and you are reading these last words about honoring Jesus, to follow these suggestions. Read and reread the four gospels over and over again. Get several different translations, and read Matthew, Mark, Luke, and John repeatedly. Paul is easier to read, but Jesus's life touches a deeper, more foundational level in the heart. Jesus is all about love. Jesus is all about becoming immersed in God's love.

Underline each statement or act of Jesus's life in the four gospels. Underline more deeply what speaks to you personally. Do not be afraid of marking up your gospels because when you come back and reread that passage, you will remember the first time it spoke to you, and the words and life of Jesus will become more alive within you. Always compare Jesus's teachings to Paul's teachings. Meditate on each sentence of Jesus and each word of Jesus. Doing this will help you to intuitively know what Jesus would do at any given moment in your life. Paul would wholeheartedly agree when you fully realize *it is all about Jesus*.

ADDENDUM 1

How the Themes in This Book Developed

The themes in this book have been developing in my mind for many years. Most of the foundational thoughts of this manuscript were written long ago and have been picked up and read and then laid back in my file cabinet for over five decades. They have been intermittently reviewed and pondered countless times. I realized after writing four previous books that these long-nurtured, strongly believed ideas needed to be thought and rethought, worked and reworked, because my initial words were far too harsh on Paul.

The message of Jesus would not today be spread across the entire planet if it had not been for this Jewish apostle who was sent to Jews and non-Jews. Paul realized he was not alone in his missionary work. He often says, "Many others," also have laid the foundational faith structure for Christians on Jesus and Jesus's life, and this has taken place for many centuries right down to this present time.

Years before this book on Paul was published, I had just concluded one of my "Introduction to the New Testament" lectures at Friends University, Topeka Campus, on the Epistles of Paul, when a young man came up after my lecture and said, "Dr. Cobb, I have been angry at Paul for years. I never liked a lot of what he wrote. Then I heard your lecture tonight, and it made sense. Thank you. I had never seen Paul in that light before. Now I understand him better. I am not as angry with him."

It was at that point that I realized I might be approaching a point when I could begin to reprocess my initial ideas and now could produce a less bombastic, angry stance and a more balanced review of Paul's life and words in relationship to Jesus of Nazareth. Paul truly felt he had a mission to bring the message of Jesus as Messiah to the non-Jewish nations of his day. Paul had tried to the very best of his considerable ability to do that. Most of the people who call themselves Christian today realize they owe their faith to this "Apostle to the Gentiles."

Not long after that conversation with my student, the September 11 attacks in New York took place, and the two World Trade Center buildings were brought down. I was called to active duty in the US Army as command chaplain (colonel) for the Thirty-Fifth Infantry Division and then later called to be command chaplain with the Thirty-Fifth Division, providing religious coverage to American soldiers on SFOR 13 rotation of NATO soldiers on their peacekeeping mission at Eagle Base in Tuzla. This took place in the Islamic nation of Bosnia-Herzegovina. There, I interacted with Bosnian Islamic leaders, Serbian Orthodox leaders, and Croatian Catholic leaders and in Sarajevo, with Jewish leaders trying to bring peace to that nation.

After retiring from thirty years in the reserve components and active duty of the US Army, I pastored a small church; began setting up my clinic, Hope for Life; and served on the board of Southeastern European Development Solutions (SEEDS). I wrote four books that were literally burning inside of me because of my life experiences at that time.

The fire of this book on the supremacy of Jesus over Paul has been smoldering even longer than the fires of those initial books. It had been growing for over five long decades deep within me throughout all those years. From thoroughly studying the words of Paul for years, I absolutely know that *Paul would deeply approve of my attempt to lift up the name and life of Jesus of Nazareth much, much higher than that of Paul of Tarsus.*

On December 25, 1982, I was talking with a PhD student from the University of Chicago. He said that both Lenin and Marx would be greatly disturbed if they came back from the dead and saw what has been done in their name. I believe that such is the case with Paul of Tarsus. If Paul came back from the dead, he would see that far too many of Jesus's followers have overly lionized Paul at the expense of Jesus, whom Paul loved and served with all his strength, intellect, life, and very blood.

Early on in my Christian walk, I had become increasingly disturbed during Roman Catholic Masses, Protestant worship services, and adult Sunday school classes and Bible studies. I was repeatedly hearing priests, pastors, Bible teachers, and Christian leaders say, "Jesus said," and then directly quote from an epistle of Paul of Tarsus.

Taylor Caldwell wrote a book about Paul with the title *Great Lion of God*. It was a balanced work of fiction and fact and looked both at Paul's inspiration and at his humanity. So many people from a wide variety of Christian traditions place Paul as the only lion of God for the cause of Jesus. Paul has been lionized too much. The Great Lion of God can only be the Lion of the tribe of Judah, Jesus of Nazareth himself.

Simon, who became Peter "the Rock," was the first disciple to realize that Jesus was the Messiah. Jesus recognized Peter's solid, rock-hard personality and knew that faith like he had would be an excellent foundation to all who would later seek to understand God through the message he was bringing to the earth. Peter was a great apostle too, and the Roman Catholic Church and many other Christians rightly place Peter before Paul in importance.

I hope this book has helped you become much more aware of several things: first of the words of Jesus; second of the specific teachings of Jesus; third of the life, death, and resurrection of Jesus; and fourth, of Jesus as the Messiah, the Long Awaited One, the Son of the Living God, the Creator of the Cosmos, our Savior, and our Friend; and fifth, how Paul of Tarsus was *all about Jesus of Nazareth.*

—Ronald Lee Cobb

ADDENDUM 2

Dr. Sid Frieswyk, Clinical Psychologist and Fan of Jesus

Dr. Sid Frieswyk was the senior psychologist when I was the senior addiction therapist at Menninger Psychiatric Hospital and working in the Professionals in Crisis program. In the six years I worked there, several Menninger patients who previously met with Sid then met with me. They said, "What you are telling me is exactly what Dr. Frieswyk told me." As this happened time after time, I moved from being startled to realizing that Sid obviously shared my core belief system about Jesus of Nazareth and my basic thoughts on recovery, spirituality, psychotherapy, and ethical behavior.

After the World Trade Center towers were destroyed on September 11, I was called to active duty in the US Army and never had the chance to speak at length with Sid individually. After I retired from the army and began my own clinic, I started attending the Men's Book Study Group at Grace Cathedral in Topeka. It was well worth the one-way thirty-mile drive there every Thursday morning at seven in the morning.

Sid was a regular attendant at that the group. I got to know him well. I told him I was working on this book about the supremacy of Jesus and how Paul of Tarsus had always tried to be an obedient servant to Jesus of Nazareth. This is not to diminish the powerful ministries of the twelve Jewish apostles and the Jewish women who followed Jesus.

I shared my great concern that Paul was too often the topic of homilies, worship messages, meditations, and publications and that Jesus was far too often placed in a secondary role in many Eastern Orthodox, Roman Catholic, and Protestant settings. I knew from Sid's previous comments that he was very much centered on the life and teachings of Jesus of Nazareth.

Here are Sid's comments. I have his permission to share them with you:

> I am deeply moved by what you say. Yet I am not at all surprised. I think we share a bond of love that in the Life of the Christ was manifest in His self-sacrifice and in His devotion to the well-being of children, the vulnerable, the unfortunate, the sick, and the lame, but mostly to those who wander through life unsure of a path that makes sense. He created loving connections with others who do not know themselves nor how to reach out to build intimacy, trust, commitment, and compassion with one another.

It is true that I loved the Roman/Latin Mass. It was a shock and a tearful disappointment for me to revisit St. Josephs Parish in West Orange New Jersey to see how small it was and to confront the reality that the mystic rituals and language of Rome were gone. I left in tears. Fathers Glover, Cunningham, and Trainor are still in my mind. My affection for them and leprosy. The liturgy is gone.

Now distilled in my life is the compassion of Christ who embraced us all not to condemn but to inspire hope in a life free from the savagery imposed on us by our brutish origins in evolution. Genesis is a lovely illusion that it is we who failed to follow God's implicit commandment to remain as innocent children forever obedient to the commandments of our parents from the earliest days of paradise in the embrace of mother.

The reality is that our moral failings are the residuals of evolution reflected in our neuroanatomy and the never ending clash of the primitive instincts of the jungle with the demands of family life and beyond that we love and cherish each other for the sake of our communities. It seems improbable that some would acknowledge life in which the top predator gets to keep everything including the lives of his subordinates. Jesus made abundantly clear that a loving community is concerned with the well-being of each of us no matter how marginalized, no matter how vulnerable, no matter how abhorrent they might seem, even with leprosy.

Mary Magdalen is a very interesting character that in Jesus Christ Superstar unveils what Roman Catholicism suppresses and condemns, "He's just a man; he's just a man. I've had so many men before. In very many ways he's just one more. Should I bring him down? Should I scream and shout? Should I speak of love? Let my feelings out? I never thought I'd come to this. What's it all about?"

Christ is lost in our theologies, moral and otherwise, that denude Him of His humanity reframed in Roman Catholic Moral Theology as an ideal celibacy. I will never forget the very pretty young blonde who changed my life when I confronted her in a soda shop in Jordan, Minnesota. At that point I was in a novitiate for the CSC (The Congregation of Holy Cross, a missionary congregation of priests and brothers founded in 1837 by Basil Moreau, in Le Mans, France) on the road to the minor vows and later to poverty, chastity, and obedience surrendering my humanity to Christ as demanded in the life of a monk.

Father Craddick, the novice master, had given us each a quarter and told us to go downtown to "spend it all." I saw the pretty young blonde and was startled, saying to myself, "I can't do this." I tearfully went to confession to unveil my plight and left. On the way home on a TWA flight I was surrounded by pretty young stewardesses solicitously concerned with this young man clinging to his prayer book. They were only more "occasions of sin" to which I would succumb even more passionately when I met my wife to be.

Roman Catholic moral theology has become an inhumane beast that even further alienates me amidst the plague of pedophilia that Pope Francis cannot remedy. How has the Life of the Christ become so perverted? As a psychotherapist I have seen many versions of that tragic reality. Nonetheless, beyond the disillusioning exposure to the failures of Roman Catholicism is still the spirit of the priesthood, the loving embrace of our humanity and the profound and compassionate interest in the well-being of even the least of us.

Yes, you and I are on the same path seeking the same goals to bring compassion and love to those who wander through life alone and defeated and lost. The faith that remains with me is the Love of the Christ and deep compassion for the lost and confused and tormented.

Last evening as I was engaged with a group of Chinese mental health professionals in Beijing via ZOOM it was profoundly clear that we are brothers and sisters in the same order of compassion, concern, and commitment to the well-being of each person we encounter in our professional lives. It was a group with playful language and governance. I felt honored to be included so playfully and affectionately. I was "with" them in the spirit of the Christ speaking as a psychoanalyst who cares and is devoted to the life of each who seeks our help. Shalom, Sid

ADDENDUM 3

The 1492 CE Migration of Jews from Spain to Sarajevo

Much has been said about Paul's Jewish background, the Jewish church in Jerusalem, anti-Semitism, and other Jewish issues in Christianity. The following facts from world history and my own personal insights and realizations might be helpful for you to think about as you ponder Paul, Judaism, and Jesus of Nazareth.

When I was the command chaplain of the SFOR 13 NATO Peacekeeping Mission, part of my duties sent me to visit the remaining synagogue in the capital city of Bosnia-Herzegovina. Before Hitler's arrest and persecution of the Jews, there had been four synagogues in Sarajevo. The minute I entered the city of Sarajevo, I felt right at home. I was surprised.

Sarajevo had been the epicenter of the battles and ethnic cleansing of the Serbian Orthodox Serbs against the Islamic Bosnians, and I had expected to feel uneasy, disturbed, and the other negative emotions I had often felt in other battle zones, but I did not. Sarajevo felt familiar. It felt like I had been there before. It took me weeks to understand what was going on inside me. Then I realized what it was.

I had grown up in Santa Barbara, California. In grade school, they taught us songs in Spanish. The Spanish architecture of Santa Barbara was familiar to me. It felt comforting. I had Hispanic friends and was familiar with Latin and people speaking Spanish in my presence.

The Roman Catholicism in every Franciscan church I entered in California had a distinct Spanish twist not only with architecture but within the culture itself. Why was Sarajevo so like Spain?

I discovered that when England had driven the Jews out in the thirteenth century and Spain had driven them out in the fifteenth century, moderate Islamic nations had welcomed them. Islamic people knew that a big part of their faith was taken from Jewish roots. The Ottoman Empire in Sarajevo welcomed the Jews.

In Medina, where Mohammed had fled from attempted murder in Mecca, Jews there had welcomed him, given him aid, and eventually chosen him to be the commander and head of the Medina city-state. When Mohammed first came to Medina, there were five tribes there. Two tribes were Arabic, and three of the tribes were Jewish. The Jewish tribes had fled there from Judah and Jerusalem after the Romans had destroyed Jerusalem in 70 CE.

Later, in 1492 CE, thousands of Jews who had owned businesses or were merchants or educators in Spain had descended on Sarajevo en masse. There originally were four synagogues before the Croatians and the Nazis decimated the Jewish community. Only one remained.

The Jews from Spain had set up shops and schools and continued developing their regional and international business interests. For three hundred years, the trade language in Sarajevo was Spanish. Much of the architecture the Spanish Jews brought was Spanish. No wonder I felt at home there.

The wise Jewish lay leader in the remaining synagogue (it was not large enough to have a Rabbi) had relatives who had moved from Sarajevo to the United States before the terrible war of aggression by the Serbian Christians against the mostly unarmed Islamic Bosnians began. The Sarajevo Jews had been caught essentially in a second ethnic cleansing, except this time, it was against the Islamic peoples and not the Jews.

His plea with a kind smile and gentle words to me were "Please always leave a few Americans in Bosnia when your forces go home. With a few of you here, the Serbs will never again begin again to slaughter us." I am pleased to say that someone in the State Department had listened to his plea, and a few American military advisors are still in Sarajevo.

ADDENDUM 4

Paul the Servant and How
He Was All about Jesus

You'll remember, friends, that when I first came to you to let you in on God's master stroke, I didn't try to impress you with polished speeches and the latest philosophy. I deliberately kept it plain and simple: first Jesus and who he is; then Jesus and what he did—Jesus crucified. (I Corinthians 2:2 MSG)

I bring this up because some from Chloe's family brought a most disturbing report to my attention—that you're fighting among yourselves! I'll tell you exactly what I was told: You're all picking sides, going around saying, "I'm on Paul's side," or "I'm for Apollos," or "Peter is my man," or "I'm in the Messiah group."

I ask you, "Has the Messiah been chopped up in little pieces so we can each have a relic all our own? Was Paul crucified for you? Was a single one of you baptized in Paul's name?" I was not involved with any of your baptisms—except for Crispus and Gaius—and on getting this report, I'm sure glad I wasn't. At least no one can go around saying he was baptized in my name. (Come to think of it, I also baptized Stephanas's family, but as far as I can recall, that's it.)

God didn't send me out to collect a following for myself, but to preach the Message of what he has done, collecting a following for him. And he didn't send me to do it with a lot of fancy rhetoric of my own, lest the powerful action at the center—Christ on the Cross—be trivialized into mere words. (I Corinthians 1:11–17 MSG)

We each carried out our servant assignment. I planted the seed, Apollos watered the plants, but God made you grow. It's not the one who plants or the one who waters who is at the center of this process but God, who makes things grow. Planting and watering are menial servant jobs at minimum wages. What makes them worth doing is the God we are serving. You happen to be God's field in which we are working.

To put it another way, you are God's house. Using the gift God gave me as a good architect, I designed blueprints; Apollos is putting up the walls. Let each carpenter who comes on the job take care to build on the foundation! Remember, there is only one foundation, the one already laid: Jesus Christ*. (I Corinthians 3:5–11 MSG)*

ADDENDUM 5

Ben Gerardy, a Catalyst to Writing about Paul of Tarsus

Ben Gerardy was my hero when I was a young pastor almost fifty years ago. He was the associate regional minister of the Christian Church in Kansas (Disciples of Christ). He had been a US Army chaplain in Vietnam. One day in a combat zone, his helicopter had been shot down. No one was seriously injured.

When they hit the ground and pulled themselves out of the wreckage, a soldier looked at Ben, saw the chaplain cross on his uniform, and said, "So that is why we are alive." At the time, I was a young Army National Guard chaplain, and Ben's combat experience and his faith in God resonated with me. I went on to spend thirty years as a US Army chaplain in the reserve components and on active duty.

I told Ben that I was worried that I was hearing about Paul of Tarsus and his teachings much more than I was hearing about Jesus of Nazareth and that I wanted to write a book correcting this overemphasis on Paul and underemphasis on Jesus. Ben just laughed at me dismissively. He laughed at my concern.

Months later at a denominational meeting, he derisively asked me in the presence of another church leader, "Writing your book yet?" Again, he jokingly dismissed me, and both of them laughed derogatively and walked away. I'm sure Ben thought I was young, far too arrogant, and way too proud to even think of taking on someone like Paul.

I don't think Ben fully understood that my main concern was that Paul was often being honored more than Jesus of Nazareth. I'm not sure Ben and many other Christians are fully aware of the fact that keeping Jesus first was also Paul's very real concern. Paul desperately wanted Jesus to be honored. Later, Ben again asked me the same dismissive question: "How's that book coming?" His jokes hurt, but Ben was a needed catalyst. He spurred me on to think more intently for the past fifty years on this issue. I sincerely want to say, "Thank you, Ben Gerardy, for being in my life." Honest friends can be incredibly helpful.

ADDENDUM 6

Tolstoy's Total Dedication to Jesus of Nazareth

Another catalyst in writing this book emphasizing Jesus was the life of Tolstoy and later the life of Alexander Solzhenitsyn. Count Leo Tolstoy was totally dedicated to Jesus of Nazareth in his later years. As a wealthy member of the Russian nobility and a landowner, Tolstoy was a nominal follower of Jesus and grew up in the Russian Orthodox Church. As a young man, he took advantage of the peasants who worked his land, but over the years, his faith in Jesus of Nazareth changed his life. He began treating his peasants as family and became caring and kind—more and more like Jesus of Nazareth. For Tolstoy, *it was all about Jesus*.

Tolstoy eventually denounced the Russian Orthodox Church. Before the Russian Revolution of 1917, it had become a tool of the czar and the Russian government, he believed, and had lost its emphasis on Jesus of Nazareth. He wanted nothing to do with organized Russian state religion.

Alexander Solzhenitsyn disagreed with Tolstoy. While Solzhenitsyn agreed that the church had become corrupt, he disagreed that it was no longer viable. Solzhenitsyn believed that imperfect as it was, the church was still able to carry the message of Jesus to the next generation.

Solzhenitsyn had initially been an atheist when fighting the Germans in World War II as a major in the Russian Field Artillery. Stalin had pulled him off the front lines and sent him to the notorious Russian prison system known as the Gulag Archipelago. Solzhenitsyn had sent a letter to a friend in Moscow joking innocuously about Stalin, Stalin's secret police had read that letter, and he was immediately thrown into prison still in his military uniform.

In the solitude of twelve years of prison, quietly watching dedicated Russian Orthodox believers quote from memory the liturgy of Communion and sing from their hearts the hymns of the Orthodox faith they had memorized from childhood changed Solzhenitsyn. Their lives honored Jesus of Nazareth to the point where he changed from an atheist to a follower of Jesus.

After so many years in prison, Solzhenitsyn realized it is all about Jesus, just as Tolstoy had realized years before Communism. To this very day and even when atheistic Communism ruled Russia for seventy years, young men and women would travel to Tolstoy's old estate, which had become a preserved historical site, and stand by his grave for their marriage ceremony. Tolstoy is a great hero in Russia in part because he *realized it was all about Jesus.*

ADDENDUM 7

Thoughts on Writing the Words of This Book

Some books make us free.
—Ralph Waldo Emerson

I would be a liar ... to say
That I don't write for the reader.
I do. But for the reader who hears,
Who will really work for it.
—Maya Angelou

Every burned book
Enlightens the world.
—Ralph Waldo Emerson

Your word "focus" is so accurate.
Most people go through life unfocused.
The secret of life
And the secret of serenity
Is becoming more and

More focused
Every day.
—Ronald Lee Cobb

Lord, help us to keep an unbroken focus on
You, our shepherd, even in the midst of
All the distractions that get in our way.
—John Dillworth

ADDENDUM 8

The Quakers, the Baptists, and Paul of Tarsus

I had finished my master's of divinity thesis at Central Baptist Theological seminary on "George Fox and his Contributions to Seventeenth-Century Quaker Life and Thought." I felt the Quakers were missing something, so I wrote an article in an effort to spiritually balance out the Quaker stance. The article was published in the 1974 edition of the *Baptist Journal of History and Theology*.

My article was on the details of the "Quaker-Baptist Controversy" in seventeenth-century England. The Quakers insisted that the most important thing was the Inner Light. The Baptists insisted that the Bible was the most important thing. The conclusion of my article was that both were important equally, the Inner Light and the Bible. I thought I had solved my spiritual dilemma at that time.

I was wrong. As I've grown wiser in my faith, I have discovered another, more supreme value. My understanding gradually grew and recently even more exponentially increased in my Christian faith. It is the same theme that is in every one of the letters and speeches of Paul of Tarsus. It is the central theme in all the writings and lives of Simon Peter and of the beloved John, the apostle of love.

What is the central theme that was missing in my thinking, life, and thesis? Was it missing the Inner Light or Bible emphasis? No, it was missing the most important thing. The Christian life is all about Jesus. Everything in Paul's writings and in the New Testament point to Jesus of Nazareth. It is *all about Jesus*.

ADDENDUM 9

A Spiritual Experience in Malta

My thirty-five-year-old daughter, Elizabeth, died suddenly on July 23, 2018. Her memorial service was a few days later, and my friends, her son Devin, and some of his family went with me to scatter her ashes on the family ranch. A few days later, my wife, Kathleen, and I flew to Malta. I had scheduled this flight weeks before to do research on Paul of Tarsus. Paul had been shipwrecked in Malta and had to stay there for ninety days. He had a remarkable ministry in Malta on his way to his death in Rome.

I knew that Elizabeth would have wanted me to go on this trip after her funeral service and that it was best for me in my grief to go and to continue on with my life. We landed in Frankfort and then took off for Malta. Our plane had just flown over Italy when Elizabeth's spirit came to me. "Dad, I'm okay. I'm all right."

It was beyond question that it was Elizabeth who had said those healing words to me. Her words gave me peace. We traveled all over the island, and I was able to make rough drafts of several of the chapters in this book in the beautiful port city of Valletta, Malta, because of that.

When I arrived home, I told a close friend, Lori Lindsey, how Elizabeth had come to me on the airplane. Then Lori told me her story. "When you were in Malta, I asked God to send Bobby to me and tell me how he and Elizabeth were doing."

Bobby, a close friend and Lori's husband, had died a year earlier. He called me his older brother. Bobby and Lori both knew Elizabeth. "Nothing happened for three days after I asked God to send me Bobby. Then I was outside on a still day and a feather softly landed on my lap. Then a butterfly came and landed on my shoulder and stayed there. Then Bobby spoke to me and said, 'Elizabeth and I are fine. We are all right.' When you said what Elizabeth had said to you on the airplane, the hair on my arms stood up. Bobby had told me exactly the same thing Elizabeth had told you."

I have found that when God speaks, he later confirms everything he has previously said. I pray this story about Elizabeth, Malta, and Lori blesses you and helps you realize you are never abandoned; you are a child of God, because *it is all about Jesus.*

ABOUT THE AUTHOR

Ronald Lee Cobb has been an ordained Christian minister (Disciples of Christ) for over half a century. He received his doctor of ministry from San Francisco Theological Seminary, his master of arts degree from the University of Kansas's Religious Studies Department, his master of divinity degree from Central Baptist Theological Seminary, and his Bachelor's degree from Westmont College. The motto of Westmont College is "Christus Primatum Tenens," or *Holding Christ First*, which is a foundational theme of this book on the life of Paul of Tarsus.

Ron has done postdoctoral studies at Topeka State Psychiatric Hospital, Topeka VA Hospital, Menninger Psychiatric Hospital, Princeton University, Command and General Staff College, the Naval Postgraduate School for International Relations, and the University of Virginia Medical Center. He was a chaplain (colonel) in the United States Army, retiring after thirty years.

He is a licensed clinical addiction counselor (LCAC) and can train entry-level counselors. He was the senior addiction therapist at the Menninger Psychiatric Hospital. He has served seven congregations and has led education for ministry four-year courses for the University of the South for three decades. These excellent courses include the following: year one, the Hebrew scriptures; year two, the Christian scriptures; year three, church history; and year four, how to be a Christian in the twenty-first century.

He has taught at the Disciples of Christ college in Lynchburg, Virginia; Friends University Topeka Campus; and Highland Community College and led courses in the Karl Menninger School of Psychiatry. He has also spoken at Boston University and the University of Kansas Religious Studies Department. He is the author of numerous articles and four previous books: *Memories of Bosnia: The 35th Division's SFOR 13 NATO Peacekeeping Mission* (2004); *Islam, What You Need to Know in the Twenty-First Century, a Primer for Peace* (2011); *Spiritual Journeys: Life, Miracles, Power, and Love* (2014); and *Fun and Laugher in Recovery, Otherwise, Why Recover?* (2016). He is currently the clinical director of Hope for Life (HFL) pastoral counseling clinic in Northeast Kansas and serves as pastor of Horton First Christian Church (Disciples of Christ).

Ron enjoys raising a small herd of cattle on his La Tierra de la Paz Ranch in the Little Osage River Valley, Kansas, and canoeing the beautiful rivers of the Ozark Mountains in southern Missouri and northern Arkansas with friends. He finds healing in seeing majestic bald eagles, deer, flocks of geese, and other wildlife with his locally known artist wife,

Kathleen, at their home next to Banner Creek Lake, Holton, Kansas. As you read this book, something will begin taking place in your life. May you continue to experience a paradigm shift, and may your life evermore become *all about Jesus.*

Printed in the United States
By Bookmasters